SMART
Teen Money

How to Build Confidence, Make Better Choices, and Create a Financial Future You'll Be Proud Of

By Amanda Cassar,
MFP, C.Dec, SSA™ SAPEPAA™

The information contained in this book is general in nature and provided for educational purposes only. It does not constitute personal financial advice and does not take into account your individual objectives, financial situation, or needs. Readers should seek guidance from a qualified professional for advice tailored to their circumstances.

First published 2026

Published by Amanda Cassar
Queensland, Australia

Printed in Australia

Editing: Ruth Fae | Fae Blood Publications
Cover and Interior Design: Captured by KC Designs

A catalogue record for this book is available from the National Library of Australia.

ISBN: 978-1-7645882-0-1
Ebook: 978-1-7645882-1-8

Disclaimer: Important Information

This book has been written for educational purposes only and provides general information about money, financial systems, and decision-making. It does not take into account your personal objectives, financial situation, or needs and should not be relied upon as personal financial, legal, or tax advice.

The information in this book is based on Australian laws, systems, and practices as at the time of writing. Financial rules, regulations, and legislation can change, and some information may become outdated over time.

Before making any financial decisions that could affect your future, you should consider whether the information is appropriate for your circumstances and, where necessary, seek advice from a licensed financial adviser, accountant, or other qualified professional.

While care has been taken to ensure the accuracy of the information presented, the author and publisher accept no responsibility for any loss or damage arising from reliance on the content of this book.

Some topics in this book may involve decisions that require parental or guardian involvement, particularly for readers under 18.

Dedication

*For my gorgeous grandchildren,
Hayden and Athena:*

*May your futures be bright, confident,
and financially fearless.*

*And for every young person taking their
first steps toward independence:*

You've got this.

Foreword

Money is one of those curious forces in life. It's invisible most of the time, yet it quietly shapes opportunities, confidence, choices, and freedom. Strangely, something so powerful rarely comes with clear instructions.

This book exists because many young people are expected to figure money out on their own. Parents do their best, but life is busy and the world has changed quickly. Digital money, scams, social pressure, and endless noise make it harder than ever to know what really matters.

SMART Teen Money is designed to give you the handbook many people wish they had received earlier. It brings together the lessons about earning, saving, spending, protecting, and planning that help build a strong foundation for adult life.

Think of it as the practical guide to money that sits alongside the advice parents hope to pass on but sometimes don't have the time, tools, or words to explain.

Whether you're earning your first dollar or starting to imagine your future career, the ideas in these pages aim to give you clarity, confidence, and independence so that money becomes a tool that supports your life rather than something that controls it.

Author's Note

Money can feel like a complicated adult thing that is wrapped in big words and hidden rules. But here's the truth I want you to carry from the very start:

Money isn't about spreadsheets.
It's about freedom.
Choices.
Confidence.
Breathing room.
And building a life that feels like yours.

Most of us never learned this at school. And most adults are still trying to figure it out as they go. So if you sometimes feel overwhelmed by money, not behind, you're exactly where you're meant to be.

Today more than ever, you live in a world of instant answers. You can Google anything, watch endless videos, and ask apps, influencers, algorithms, even artificial intelligence, for advice in seconds.

That's powerful. But it's also risky, especially if you don't know how to question what you're given.

This book isn't here to compete with or replace technology. It's here to help you use tools wisely and without handing over your judgement. Information may be easy to find, but good decisions are not.

This book isn't here to lecture you. It's here to help you learn how to think clearly about money, and how to pause, question, reflect, and choose.

You don't need to be good at maths.
You don't need to know everything.
You don't need to copy anyone else's version of success.

You just need curiosity, self-awareness, and the confidence to ask better questions—of the world, of advice, and of yourself.

That's what the **SMART** approach is really about. Throughout this book, you'll learn practical skills like how to earn, spend, save, invest, protect yourself, and plan ahead. But, just as importantly, you'll learn how to:

- sanity-check advice
- recognise pressure and manipulation
- tell the difference between facts and opinions
- understand trade-offs
- make decisions that align with your values, not just trends

Future You will thank you for every one of those skills.

Let's start building the life you want, one smart choice at a time.

Amanda.

How To Use This Book

This book is designed to help you build practical money skills step by step.

Each chapter introduces a key idea about how money works, followed by simple examples and actions you can take right away. Throughout the book you'll also find short quotes and reflections that highlight important ideas about habits, decision-making, and financial wellbeing.

At the end of the book, the *30-Day SMART Challenge* gives you a practical way to start applying what you've learned.

You don't need to read the book all at once. Take it chapter by chapter, think about how each idea applies to your life, and focus on building small habits that will support your future.

TABLE OF CONTENTS

CHAPTER 1

SMART BEGINNINGS

"Success is the product of daily habits, not once-in-a-lifetime transformations."

—James Clear

SMART Beginnings: Understand Money Without Overwhelm

> *"Your future is built one small choice at a time."*

Money affects almost every part of life: where you live, how you work, what opportunities you can say yes to, and how safe you feel when things go wrong. Yet most people grow up without anyone ever explaining the basics. Not because the adults are hiding the secrets, but because they were never taught either.

Money can feel big, complicated, secretive, or even a bit awkward to talk about. Sometimes it's treated like a "grown-up" topic. Sometimes it's taboo. Sometimes it feels like something you're supposed to magically "get" one day.

But here's the truth no one tells you in school:

You don't need to know everything about money. You just need to understand a few important things really well.

So, if money sometimes feels confusing or overwhelming, that's totally normal.

This book exists to make everything clearer, calmer, and far easier. And don't worry, you don't need to like maths, own a briefcase and cardigan, or suddenly become an accountant.

Money is about choices, mindset, and habits far more than it is about numbers. It's about building confidence that will follow you through school, your first job, your first pay, and every decision after that.

Money is part of life. Understanding it early in life doesn't just help your bank account, it helps your freedom and choices, your future opportunities, and even your wellbeing.

You're here now.
You're starting early.
This already puts you ahead.

WHY MONEY CAN FEEL CONFUSING

Money gives you options to move, study, travel, and breathe a little easier. It protects you during tough times and supports you during exciting ones.

Money can help you:

- build confidence
- avoid unnecessary stress
- pursue opportunities
- take care of yourself
- help others when you choose to
- design a life that feels like yours

It's true that money doesn't create happiness, but it does give you space to create a life where happiness has room to grow. And here's something that I hope is reassuring: Many adults struggle with money, not because they're bad with it, but because:

- no-one taught them properly
- they learned too late
- they learned through stress rather than guidance

- they copied what everyone else did
- they felt embarrassed to ask questions

You're doing something different because you're starting with knowledge instead of confusion. That changes everything.

HOW THIS BOOK WILL HELP

Most people fall into one of these traps:

1. **"I'll learn about money later."** Later becomes years. Sometimes decades.
2. **"I'm just bad with money."** You're not. You simply don't have the right framework yet.
3. **"Money is stressful, so I avoid it."** Avoidance always costs more than attention. Always.
4. **"Everyone else seems to know what they're doing."** They don't. They're guessing too.

This book gives you the foundation most people wish they'd had from the start.

By the end, you'll know how to:

- understand how money works
- earn more confidently
- spend wisely without missing out
- save without stress or guilt
- invest calmly and safely
- avoid scams and online traps
- plan for the life you want
- feel secure, not overwhelmed

You don't have to be "good with numbers." You just need to be curious enough to start.

STARTING YOUNG IS YOUR SUPERPOWER

Learning to manage your money is not about perfection, or restriction, or becoming an overnight budgeting guru. Being good with money comes down to one simple thing: understanding how money flows and learning to direct that flow with intention.

Small choices, repeated consistently, can entirely change your financial direction. The SMART approach gives you clarity and confidence—and that's exactly what you need!

Money grows with time, not luck. A tiny amount saved or invested now can become a surprisingly big amount later because of something called **compounding** (don't worry, we'll get to that).

Starting early gives you:

- more choices
- less stress
- more confidence
- stronger habits
- a huge head start compared to most adults

Future You will look back and be glad you began now.

REAL TALK

Most people don't think about money until they're forced to. You're choosing to learn early. That is rare, and powerful.

MONEY IS NOT ABOUT "BEING RICH"

Money isn't about showing off or having the trendiest things. When you strip away all the noise, money is about:

- security
- options
- freedom
- flexibility
- the ability to help others
- the confidence to make decisions
- a future that feels stable

And those things matter more than any brand name.

THE WAY YOU THINK ABOUT MONEY MATTERS

Everyone has a "money story"—the things they heard growing up that shaped how they feel about it today. Your parents will have their own money stories, too. You might have heard:

"Money is stressful."
"We can't afford that."
"You have to work hard to get ahead."
"Money doesn't grow on trees."
"People with money are greedy."
"Money is the root of all evil."

None of these are universally true. They're simply stories passed down from one generation to the next. This book helps you build your *own* story, one that is based on clarity, confidence, and calm.

THE GOAL OF SMART TEEN MONEY

The goal is progress over perfection. Having clarity rather than being strict. And feeling confident with your money, not fearful that you will make mistakes. Money should make your life easier. You don't need to be brilliant with money, you simply need a system you trust.

SMART TIP

Small steps done consistently beat big steps done rarely.

THE SMART APPROACH

This series is called SMART for a reason. Every chapter is designed to build:

SECURITY—knowing your basics, building buffers, and protecting yourself.

MINDSET—understanding how you think about money, and shaping healthier habits.

AWARENESS—tracking where money goes, recognising traps, and learning how systems work.

RESILIENCE—preparing for surprises, and developing a calm, confident approach to challenges.

TOOLS—practical strategies, systems, and actions you can use immediately.

This book will teach you how to manage money in real-life.

Understanding money isn't about collecting quick answers. Today you can search almost anything and get an instant response from a video, an influencer, a website, or even artificial intelligence. But an answer isn't the same as understanding. An answer tells you what someone else thinks. Understanding helps you decide what's right for you. Throughout this book, you'll learn not just the "what" of money, but the "why" and the "what if," so you can make decisions with confidence rather than simply following the loudest voice.

THIS IS YOUR TOOLKIT, NOT A RULEBOOK

You can use this book in whatever way works for you:

- Read it from start to finish
- Jump to sections that matter right now
- Skim it
- Highlight it
- Use the checklists, tips, and activities
- Come back to chapters later

There is no wrong way to learn about money.

Money is personal and so is the way you learn it. You'll notice:

- short paragraphs
- simple explanations
- stories and examples
- visual anchors
- SMART Tips
- Real Talk boxes
- Warnings where you need them
- step-by-step tools
- easy mini activities

These are here to make learning easier, lighter, and feel less like homework. You can read this on the bus, between classes, at home, or in tiny bursts before bed. Every minute counts.

A NEW WAY TO THINK ABOUT MONEY

Money isn't the villain. It's not the source of all evil; apparently, that's the LOVE of money. But then, it isn't the hero either. Money is a tool. It's neutral, flexible, and responsive, and when you know how to use it well, it becomes one of the most empowering parts of your life.

You don't need to become obsessed. You just need to become aware.

And by the end of this book, you'll understand:

- how money works
- how to make it last
- how to build savings that feel achievable
- how to invest without fear
- how to protect yourself from scams
- how to navigate tech, algorithms, and spending traps
- how to build a financial plan that fits your life

You don't need to manage your money perfectly from the beginning, you just need to start. And by reading this book, you're already doing that.

WHAT'S NEXT?

So... you've started thinking about money. That already puts you ahead of a *lot* of adults. Now comes the mystery many of us experience: **Why does money sometimes feel like it disappears the moment you get it?**

In **Chapter 2—SMART Money Flows: Understand the Basics Without the Boring Bits**, we follow your money around and see what it's doing when you're not watching.

No budgets yet.

No spreadsheets lurking in the shadows. And never any judgement.

Just understanding:

- where money comes from
- where it tends to leak out
- why some people always seem "fine" on the same income
- how understanding the flow makes everything else easier

Once you see how money moves, any confusion you feel will lessen and making smarter choices will feel natural. Lights on. Fog gone.

CHAPTER 2

SMART MONEY FLOWS

"Give every dollar a job."

—Jesse Mecham

SMART Money Flows: Understand the Basics Without the Boring Bits

> *"Money is a tool. Learn to use the tool, and you can build anything you want."*

Money can feel mysterious until you understand the simple way it moves in and out of your life. Right now, it may feel unpredictable, a bit like Melbourne weather with its "four seasons in one day." Once you understand the pattern, it stops feeling random. Money doesn't have to be complicated, it's just not always well explained. Once you see how money *flows*, everything else—earning, spending, saving, investing—suddenly clicks.

Most adults never learn this. But you're about to understand it in one chapter.

No spreadsheets. No lectures. No yawns. Let's make money feel less like a puzzle and more like a map.

Before you can make smart decisions with money, it helps to understand how money moves through your life.

Money is always doing one of three things: coming in, going out, or getting stuck in the middle. Sadly, there's no secret fourth option where it magically behaves.

Most people only focus on the, "How do I get more?" part, but the real power comes when you understand the whole flow. This chapter gives you a clear picture of that flow so you can take control of it, instead of feeling like it's controlling you.

MONEY COMES IN: WAYS YOU EARN

Income isn't just a salary. It can come from dozens of places:

- an allowance
- part-time or casual work
- freelance or side-hustle jobs
- selling items you no longer use
- gifts like birthday money
- small business ideas
- creative income (art, editing, tutoring)
- bonuses or commissions
- government payments
- investments (later in life)

Your income is fuel, but the amount matters less than what you do with it. More fuel helps, sure, but direction here matters more than speed because small amounts handled well, will go further than big amounts handled badly. (You'll see this play out again and again.)

WHERE MONEY COMES FROM: 3 TYPES OF INCOME

1. Active Income

You work and you get paid. This includes casual jobs, babysitting, coaching, yard work, tutoring, shifts, side gigs.

More work = more money.
Stop work = money stops.

2. Passive Income

Your money works for you. This includes investing, interest, rental income, or selling something digital.

You set it up once, and it earns over time. It might be small at first, and possibly feel a bit boring. Then it can become impressive. Money grows surprisingly quickly when you stay consistent. And this can often make you wish you'd started sooner.

3. Future Income

This includes superannuation and retirement income; money you won't touch until later in life but grows in the background for decades. This is a slow, powerful type of income that Adult You will be thankful for.

Understanding these three helps you build a balanced money life.

WHY YOU WANT MORE THAN ONE STREAM OF INCOME

Relying on one source of money is like standing on one leg; it's fine for a moment or two, but risky for the long term. If something happens, like you lose hours at work, can't take shifts, or school becomes intense, the whole thing wobbles.

But with two or three small income streams?

You're steady.
You're stronger.
You have options.

Multiple small incomes can be safer than one big one.

> **SMART TIP**
>
> *You don't need more money—you need better flow.*

MONEY GOES OUT

Spending falls into two groups:

1. The Visible Stuff

You tap your card or your phone and you feel it. It's for food, drinks, clothes, transport, outings—the regular things.

2. The Invisible Stuff

This is where people get tripped up. Invisible outgoings can be:

- subscriptions
- app renewals
- bank fees
- in-app purchases
- small "treats" that add up
- late fees
- buy-now-pay-later instalments

Most people don't realise their invisible spending outweighs their visible spending. It's not the big splurges that impact our money flow, it's the quiet little taps that we don't always notice.

When you understand your spending patterns, you gain the power to redirect your money where it helps you. And whatever is *left* becomes:

- savings
- investments
- emergency funds
- opportunities
- future comfort

That's the entire financial system in straightforward terms. And while it's simple on paper, it can be trickier in real life. "Simple" doesn't mean easy, but it does give you clarity.

THE FOUR PLACES YOUR MONEY GOES

Every dollar you get ends up in one of these four places:

1. Living

Everything you need to get through the day: food, transport, school supplies, clothes, hygiene, hobbies.

2. Lifestyle

Fun stuff: outings, entertainment, gifts, treats, experiences. This is the "life is good" category.

3. Safety

Your buffer. Your emergency stash. The money that protects you from surprises.

4. Future

Savings for bigger goals. Investing. Longer-term dreams. This is the money that builds options.

Once you know where your money should go, your choices will feel less stressful.

> **REAL TALK**
>
> *Many people think they "don't have enough money to manage." But the truth is that learning to manage $20 builds the skills to manage $200... or $2,000... or $200,000.*
>
> *Small amounts teach big lessons.*

WHY MONEY FEELS LIKE IT DISAPPEARS

Money flows out faster when:

- you tap instead of pay cash
- you lose track of small purchases
- subscriptions auto-renew
- you follow your friends' spending pace
- you shop when you're bored
- you forget what's coming up (gifts, events, fees)
- you react instead of plan

Nothing is wrong with you. This is how modern spending is designed. Money unpredictability often feels personal, but it's usually environmental. Again, very Melbourne-weather energy.

Money doesn't vanish, it evaporates through tiny leaks. Slowly and quietly and while you're not looking. In the next few chapters, you'll learn how to plug the leaks.

AWARENESS IS MORE IMPORTANT THAN NUMBERS

You don't need to track every cent or build complicated spreadsheets. Before you can change anything about your money, you must *see it clearly.*

No judgement.
No shame.
Just information—and this information is power.

Try this: For just 48 hours, write down (or screenshot) every dollar that moves, whether into or out of your bank accounts. Have no explanations or guilt, just feel the clarity you are gaining. You'll be amazed by what you learn.

You simply need to know:

- What comes in
- What goes out
- Where it goes
- What your patterns look like

Once you see your patterns, you can shape them.

When you're unaware, money feels chaotic. But when you become aware, it feels manageable, even before you change anything.

ALWAYS FEEL "BROKE?"

It's usually not your income's fault. And it's probably not because you don't earn enough. It's because you:

- don't track the flow
- react instead of plan
- spend without understanding your patterns
- use money emotionally
- avoid conversations about it

The earlier you learn how to track and understand your money flow, the easier everything becomes.

UNDERSTANDING FLOW CHANGES EVERYTHING

When you understand the basic movement of money, you can:

- plan more easily
- avoid financial surprises
- stay out of unnecessary debt
- prioritise what matters
- save without it feeling difficult
- make decisions that support your future
- build confidence, one habit at a time

Money becomes less emotional and more practical—and that's incredibly freeing.

YOUR PERSONAL MONEY FLOW MAP

You're going to learn how to sketch this out:

Money comes in → flows through your buckets → fuels your goals → supports your future.

This will help to make things visible—and visibility changes behaviour fast!

Flow looks like: Earn → Spend (needs and wants) → Save → Grow → Give

You already use this flow in life, this book just helps you use it with purpose instead of by accident.

You'll refine this map as you work through the book. And remember that control doesn't come from restrictions, it comes from awareness and a few better choices repeated often.

SMART TIP

If you want to feel in control of money, follow the flow. Your choices live in the patterns.

Money follows attention. What you pay attention to grows.

THE REAL GOAL OF THIS CHAPTER

Is not to make you an expert or overwhelm you. It is simply to give you a clear picture of where money goes, and how you can direct it instead of chasing it.

Once you see the flow, you can change the flow.

That's where power begins.

WHAT'S NEXT?

Now that you understand how money *moves*, it's time to talk about how it *arrives*.

Chapter 3—SMART Earning: Build Income, Opportunities, and Confidence is about more than just getting a job and waiting for payday. It's about understanding your value, spotting opportunities, building skills, and learning how to earn in ways that grow with you.

Not "hustle culture."
Not "burnout."
Not "work harder forever."

Just smarter earning choices that give you options, confidence, and momentum.

CHAPTER 3

SMART EARNING

"Your future income depends on the habits you build today."

—Unknown

SMART Earning: Build Income, Opportunities, and Confidence

> *"The best time to start earning is when you're ready. The second-best time is now."*

Earning your own money changes how you feel about your life. It gives you independence, boosts your confidence, and teaches you things school never will. Suddenly your time feels more valuable—because it is! Your first dollars, no matter how small, are powerful because they represent:

- choice
- freedom
- growth
- responsibility
- momentum

Let's make earning something you look forward to, not something you dread.

> **SMART TIP**
>
> *Your first job teaches you more about people than any textbook ever will.*

THE FIRST STEPS INTO EARNING

Income tends to come from three places, and none of them require you to have everything figured out.

1. Part-Time or Casual Work

The classics:

- hospitality
- retail
- cinemas
- supermarkets
- fast food
- sports coaching
- lifeguarding
- babysitting or petsitting
- tutoring

These jobs teach resilience and people skills incredibly fast.

2. Side Hustles

These are flexible and creative:

- digital design and editing
- reselling clothing or baking treats
- cleaning jobs or yard work
- washing cars, gardening, or dog walking
- art commissions or selling handmade items
- helping neighbours with tech or errands

Small, simple ideas can become surprisingly profitable.

3. Micro-Work Online (Careful Here)

Doing surveys, selling photos, and using skill platforms can work but they require caution to avoid scams. If something promises easy money for almost no effort... PAUSE! Real income usually asks for *something* in return.

You'll learn how to stay safe in the scam chapters later.

Your first job doesn't define you. It's simply your starting point, your launch pad, if you like. Nobody is judging your future based on your first pay slip. What matters most is that you begin building experience, reliability, and self-trust. When you earn, you learn:

- how the world works
- how to communicate with adults
- how to manage time
- how to handle responsibility
- how to build confidence
- how to solve problems
- how to value your own effort

Earning doesn't just grow your bank account, it grows *you*.

Don't underestimate how valuable early earning is. Future You will be very glad you didn't.

> **REAL TALK**
>
> *You don't need a "real job" to earn real money. You just need a skill, a bit of initiative, and the willingness to start small. Starting small is how momentum begins... and who knows how far you'll go?*

YOUR SKILLS ARE YOUR EARNING POWER

Think about your life. Do you:

- Play a sport? → teamwork, discipline
- Study? → focus, commitment
- Help at home? → responsibility

- Tutor classmates? → communication
- Use social media well? → creativity, digital skills
- Game? → strategy, persistence, problem-solving

You're probably more skilled than you realise. Most people are; you just don't think of everyday skills as valuable—until you get paid for them! The more you use your skills, the more valuable you become in any job or side hustle.

Some people feel embarrassed about starting in retail or fast food or "at the bottom." Don't be. Everyone starts somewhere, and it's usually somewhere slightly awkward. Every financially successful adult can tell you about their first terrible job, their worst shift ever, the most bizarre customer they served, and how those early experiences shaped them

Your first job is not your forever job; it's your training ground. And who knows, it could also lead to amazing things! Many successful people started with forgettable jobs, awkward first attempts, or rejection. The difference isn't that they had pure, raw talent, it was that they kept going.

Keanu Reeves: Worked as a dishwasher and cleaner, including sweeping floors, while auditioning and being rejected early in his acting career.

Ed Sheeran: Busked on the streets, played gigs in empty rooms, slept on friends' couches, and handed out CDs himself for years before anyone noticed.

MrBeast (Jimmy Donaldson): Posted hundreds of YouTube videos that went nowhere, studied algorithms obsessively, deleted content, and started again, for years before success.

Margot Robbie: Worked at Subway, made sandwiches, and took small acting jobs while auditioning and being rejected repeatedly before landing bigger roles.

Troye Sivan: Uploaded homemade YouTube videos from his bedroom, slowly built an audience, and released early music that didn't immediately succeed.

Celeste Barber: Worked in office and admin roles while auditioning for years before her online content gained traction.

THE THREE TYPES OF EARNERS

1. The Time-Swapper: Gets paid per hour. Simple, straightforward, consistent.

2. The Problem-Solver: Gets paid to fix or improve something. Often earns more with fewer hours.

3. The Creator: Makes or designs something others want. Very flexible, often scalable.

You can be one, two, or all three. Most people move between them as life changes.

> **REAL TALK**
>
> *Most teens don't have a money problem—they have an earning opportunity they haven't recognised yet. This is good news, by the way!*

HOW TO GET YOUR FIRST JOB

Step 1: Create a simple resume

Even if you've never worked, include:

- school subjects
- sports
- volunteering
- interests
- awards
- skills (communication, teamwork, reliability)

A simple, clean resume already puts you ahead of many teens. Create a LinkedIn profile. Follow some people you know or admire and see how they put their profile together for maximum impact!

Why this matters:

A resume and LinkedIn profile help employers quickly understand who you are and what you can offer. Most employers receive many applications, even for casual jobs, so a clear profile helps you stand out.

Your resume shows your basic experience, interests and reliability. Your LinkedIn profile does something slightly different. It helps you build a professional online presence and learn how people present their skills and achievements.

Even if you have little, or no, work experience, starting early helps you practise describing your strengths and interests. Over time, you can update both as you gain new skills, qualifications and jobs.

Learning how to present yourself professionally is a skill that will benefit you throughout your life.

Step 2: Walk in and introduce yourself

A quick, polite introduction goes a long way: "Hi, I'm looking for casual work. Is there someone I can hand my resume to?"

Speak clearly. Smile. Be confident even if you don't feel confident yet. *Fake it 'til you make it!*

Step 3: Follow up

If you don't hear back, check in a week later. Persistence reads as responsibility, not pushiness.

FINDING OPPORTUNITIES OTHERS DON'T SEE

Some income streams are obvious, whereas others appear once you stop thinking you need permission to start. Look for opportunities in places like:

- local businesses needing administration or online help
- parents who want to hire a tutor for younger kids
- small businesses that need help with social media content
- neighbours looking for lawn mowing or garden help
- people who need help in setting up phones or tech
- online marketplaces (reselling, flipping, upcycling)
- petsitting or housesitting
- editing video or audio content, social media management
- digital design, Canva templates, or simple branding tasks
- event help (set-up, pack-down, photography, ushering)

Think of earning opportunities in two ways: skills you already have and skills you can learn quickly. Both are valuable. Try one at a time. Keep it simple and build slowly.

Side hustles teach creativity, communication, and responsibility—often better than school can.

THE REAL PURPOSE OF EARLY INCOME

Your first pay isn't supposed to be life changing, it's supposed to be YOU changing. This is the start of a lifelong journey. And, if you want, you can use it to teach you:

- responsibility
- confidence
- the value of time
- boundaries
- workplace behaviour
- communication
- how money flows
- how to balance life and work
- how to manage your own expectations

What you learn in your first working years can support you for decades.

> **SMART TIP**
>
> *Your skills are the engine of your future income. The more you learn and practice, the more you can earn.*
>
> *Every small job counts. Even the ones that seem boring are teaching you responsibility, confidence, and how the real world works.*

UNLOCK YOUR EARNING POTENTIAL

You grow earning power by:

- showing up
- learning new skills
- taking initiative
- being polite
- working consistently
- saying yes to opportunities
- building a reputation for reliability

These skills compound, just like money.

DIVERSIFY YOUR INCOME

Relying on one single income source used to be "normal," but today, many people enjoy having multiple, smaller streams of income, such as:

- a part-time job + tutoring
- casual work + reselling
- retail shifts + digital freelancing
- babysitting + creative commissions

This isn't hustle culture. Hustle culture pushes the idea that you should always be working and trying to earn more. Flexibility is different. It simply means having options. A small job, casual work, or a side skill can give you the freedom to earn money while still having time for school, friends, and the things you enjoy.

Your life will change over time, and your income can evolve with you.

SHOW UP WELL

No matter the job, a few habits will set you apart instantly:

Your early jobs are also where your reputation begins. The choices you make and the way you behave at work quickly shape how people see you. A strong reputation does not come from doing extraordinary things. It comes from small habits done consistently.

No matter the job, these habits will make a positive impression on your employer:

- show up on time
- communicate clearly
- ask good questions
- follow instructions
- take responsibility
- be reliable
- be willing to learn

These habits show employers that you are someone they can trust and rely on. Over time, that reputation can lead to more hours, better opportunities, and stronger references for future jobs.

HOW MUCH SHOULD YOU BE EARNING?

There's no perfect number. Anyone who tells you otherwise is guessing. Your income depends on your:

- age
- school schedule
- priorities
- mental health

- transport
- extracurricular activities
- family situation

What matters is that your income feels manageable rather than overwhelming. Even $30 a week can make a big difference when it is managed well.

HOW TO ASK FOR MORE HOURS OR BETTER SHIFTS

When asking for more hours or better shifts, the way you ask matters. Approach the conversation politely and confidently, and try to offer a practical solution rather than simply making a request.

Employers are much more likely to respond positively when they see that you are reliable, respectful and thinking about how you can help the team. For example, you might offer to cover shifts when someone is unavailable, help during busy periods, or be flexible with short notice. This approach shows that you are not just asking for something for yourself. You are showing that you are willing to contribute and support the workplace, which makes it much easier for a manager to say yes. Try:

"I'm really enjoying working here. If any extra shifts come up, I'd love to take them."
or
"I'm available on weekends or for holiday shifts if you need more coverage."

Employers remember team members who make their life easier.

AVOID BURNOUT

Watch for:

- constant tiredness
- falling marks
- losing interest in hobbies
- feeling overwhelmed
- no time for friends or rest

You are allowed to reduce your hours to prioritise school or your wellbeing. Earning money should support your life, not drain it.

Sustainable effort is far more powerful than burnout. Being constantly busy is not a badge of honour. In many cases it is a warning sign that you may be taking on too much and need to reassess your priorities.

Arianna Huffington, founder of the Huffington Post, has spoken openly about her own experience with burnout after collapsing from exhaustion. Her message is simple: *Success should not come at the cost of your health.* Learning to recognise when you need to slow down, rest, or rebalance your commitments is an important life skill. Work should be part of a healthy life, not something that overwhelms it.

SMART TIP

Money comes and goes. Your energy doesn't. Protect your energy.

UNDERSTANDING YOUR PAY

Before we go further, it helps to understand a few important terms:

Hourly Rate: What you earn for every hour you work.

Penalty Rates or Overtime: Higher pay for weekends, public holidays, late-night shifts.

Superannuation: Additional money your employer must pay into a retirement fund on top of your wage (more about this in Chapter 8).

Tax Withheld: The amount your employer sends to the ATO for you. Not a punishment, just the system at work. Knowing how it works makes it far less intimidating.

Payslip: A record of your hours, pay, tax, and super. You should receive one every pay cycle.

Understanding your payslip means you understand your rights.

YOUR EARNINGS DON'T DEFINE YOU

Work and earnings are important, but so are rest, hobbies, health, friendships, and learning. A balanced approach to earning will support you far better than burning yourself out.

Make an effort. Build your skills. But also keep room for the rest of your life. This is how your confidence will grow, and confidence is what turns earning into opportunity!

YOUR MONEY FLOW STARTS HERE

This chapter sets the foundation for everything that comes next. Once you begin earning, your money starts to flow. And when you understand how that flow works, spending, saving, growing, your whole financial life becomes easier.

CENTRELINK: OUR FINANCIAL SAFETY NET

Centrelink exists to make sure people aren't left without support during tough times. It's not designed to replace long-term income, but to act as a temporary safety net while you study, look for work, recover from illness, or get back on your feet.

For younger people, payments like Youth Allowance (for students and job seekers), Austudy (for those 25 and over who are studying), and ABSTUDY (for Aboriginal and Torres Strait Islander students) can help cover basic living costs while you work toward your future.

There are also supplementary supports such as Rent Assistance, Health Care Cards, and Crisis Payments for sudden emergencies. The key is remembering that Centrelink is a stepping stone, not a destination. It's there to help you move forward when you can—not to hold you in place—and developing your own earning capacity is still the strongest path to independence.

WHAT'S NEXT?

Now that you know how earning works—the mindset, opportunities, confidence, and value of your time—it's worth remembering that earning is only half the game. What truly shapes your financial future is what you *do* with the money once it arrives.

Some people make a little and build a lot.
Some people make a lot and build nothing.
The difference isn't luck.
It's a choice.

This is where **SMART Spending: Make Choices That Feel Good, Now and Later** comes in. This involves making decisions that feel good today *and* still support the future you're building. The way you spend money says a lot about what you value, how you think, and how much control you want over your own life.

In the next chapter, you'll learn how to spend with clarity rather than emotion, intention rather than impulse, and confidence rather than confusion.

You've learned how to earn, now let's make sure your money sticks around long enough to change your life.

SMART Earning gives you power.
SMART Spending teaches you how to use it wisely.

Let's go.

CHAPTER 4

SMART SPENDING

"The cost of anything is the amount of life you exchange for it."

—Henry David Thoreau

SMART Spending: Make Choices That Feel Good, Now and Later

> *"Enjoy your money today, but never at the expense of your future freedom."*

Spending is the fun part of money, and it's often the part everyone talks about. It's easy. It's quick. It feels good... until it suddenly doesn't. Like when you check your bank balance and get a rude shock.

Most people think spending is simple: You want something, you buy it. But *smart spending is a skill*, and once you learn it, you get something far better than new shoes or a meal out... You gain *control*. You gain *freedom*. You get the feeling of being *in charge of your life*.

Let's make spending work *for* you, not against you. You're aiming for enjoyment with control, not regret with a receipt.

REAL TALK

You're not "bad with money." You're a human living in a world built to make spending feel effortless. Effortless for you and extremely profitable for someone else.

WHY SPENDING IS SO EASY

Spending is not a bad thing. It's actually FUN, and is part of a balanced financial life.

But money moves quietly these days, via a tap on your phone, a quick autofill, or a subscription renewed silently at 2:41am. Because nothing says transparency like charging people while they're asleep. There's no pain, no pause, no moment of, "Do I actually want this?" That's not your fault; modern spending is designed to be frictionless and emotional.

Retailers hope you react rather than think, because customers who pause and consider their choices are harder to influence. Once you understand this, you gain something powerful: the ability to make your own decisions about spending rather than being pushed by advertising or impulse. And when you choose deliberately, spending can become a positive part of life. Healthy spending allows you to:

- enjoy experiences
- express your style
- take care of yourself
- celebrate wins
- invest in hobbies
- support local businesses
- build memories
- feel good about your life

Problems arise not from spending itself, but from unaware spending. Spending that isn't intentional, aligned, or considered can wreak havoc on your financial life.

This chapter builds the foundation for spending with clarity instead of impulse.

VALUES-BASED SPENDING: A BETTER FRAMEWORK

Instead of worrying about "good" or "bad" spending, try asking the question: *Does this purchase align with my values and goals?*

You may have heard people talk about "needs versus wants." The idea is simple. *Needs* are things you must have to live and function, like food, housing, transport, or basic clothing. *Wants* are the extra things that make life more enjoyable. The problem is that real life is not always that simple. Spending decisions are often more nuanced than a neat category.

Here is a better question to ask: *Does this reflect the life I am trying to build?*

If you value:

- Friends → shared meals feel meaningful
- Health → a gym membership might be worth it
- Creativity → art supplies make sense
- Independence → saving for a car makes more sense than impulse shopping

When your spending aligns with your values, you feel good. When it doesn't, you feel regret. When spending matches values, there is far less guilt and far more satisfaction. When it doesn't, regret creeps in. This chapter is about removing that regret.

THE 24-HOUR PAUSE (YOUR NEW SUPERPOWER)

If you *reeeeallly* want something... anything... wait one day.

24 hours.

When your dopamine drops and your brain switches back to logic, you'll know whether the item deserves your money.

If you still want it tomorrow, that's great!

Did you forget about it? Well, you just saved yourself from future regret. That's clarity doing its job.

THE JOY OF DELAYED GRATIFICATION

Delaying a purchase isn't about saying "no." It's about asking yourself: *Do I still want this when the emotion passes?*

Waiting 24 hours dramatically increases the quality of your purchases. You buy fewer things, but they are probably better. You save more without trying. You enjoy what you buy for longer. And you'll stop wondering where your money went.

This helps you to focus on the joy.

NEEDS, WANTS, AND YOUR "WHY"

Most financial experts talk about "needs vs. wants." That's fine, but it's not the whole story. A more insightful question is: *Why do I want this? Is it for convenience? Comfort? Confidence? Belonging? Entertainment? Boredom? Stress relief? Or habit?*

If you want "stuff" because an influencer you love told you you're unlikely to be able to live without it, you're in trouble.

Understanding the reason behind a purchase helps you decide whether it genuinely adds value or just fills a moment.

Moments are cheap. Regret isn't.

> **⚠ WARNING**
>
> *If you can't remember half your purchases, it's a sign your spending is making decisions for you, not with you.*

SPENDING PRESSURE FROM FRIENDS

You love your friends. But they can accidentally cost you a lot.

"Come on, get one too!"
"We always split evenly."
"Treat yourself!"
"It's only $20."

Most of the time it's not intentional, it's simply social.

Here are some phrases you can use to protect your money *and* your friendships:

"I'm keeping it low-cost today."
"I'll come, I just won't spend much."
"I'm saving for something big."
"I'll pay for what I ordered, not the whole split."

When you approach situations like this with short, calm, and boundaried responses, you'll find that good friends won't care. And if they do, money probably isn't the issue.

EXPERIENCES > STUFF (MOST OF THE TIME)

Clothes fade.
Tech dates.
Trendy items lose their magic fast.

But experiences like road trips, concerts, late-night chats, group dinners, memories...?

They last.
They matter.
They make you feel alive.

Spend on moments, not things. Memories age better than most purchases.

FUN DOESN'T HAVE TO BE EXPENSIVE

Some of the best life moments come from low-cost or free activities, like:

- movie nights at home
- beach days
- picnics
- thrifting adventures
- board game nights
- DIY projects
- group cooking nights
- neighbourhood walks
- creative hobbies
- free local events

People rarely regret time spent well, especially when they are hanging out with friends or family. But we often regret money spent poorly, especially when it's on things we don't remember buying! Now and then, try what the Italians call *dolce far niente*, the sweetness of doing nothing.

SUBSCRIPTIONS: THE SILENT BUDGET KILLERS

Most families now have:

- Spotify
- Netflix
- Disney+
- iCloud
- Game passes
- Editing apps
- Random trials

Individually, they are cheap. Together they can quietly turn into a very long direct debit list and a surprisingly large monthly bill.

Do a monthly subscription audit:

- ☑ Do I use it?
- ☑ Do I love it?
- ☑ Is it worth it?

Cancel anything that fails two of the three questions. Or you could choose to binge on one service at a time—then when you're sick of it, you can pause the subscription and move to another service.

And hit your mum and dad up for as long as you can. Where possible, share a family login, because paying as an additional user can be cheaper than your own service.

HOW TO AVOID EMOTIONAL SPENDING

Emotions influence spending. Always have, always will.

Shopping centres even know what music to play to make people buy more. In his 1982 study, *Using Background Music to Affect the Behavior of Supermarket Shoppers*, Ronald E. Milliman found that slower tempo music caused shoppers to move more slowly through a store and increased total sales by around 38 percent, when compared with faster music. When the researchers turned off the music for the shoppers, purchases went down.

The music influenced how long people stayed in the store, affected the buyers' emotional responses, and made them more, or less, likely to buy. As consumers, we're targeted everywhere. Stress pushes people to treat themselves. Boredom leads to scrolling and clicking. Loneliness drives "comfort shopping." Achievement sparks celebration spending. Comparison breeds impulsive purchases. Even going shopping when you're hungry can make you buy more food. Understanding this helps you to be more aware. And hopefully smarter.

Here are a few strategies to help reduce your emotional responses when shopping:

- pause before buying
- go for a walk
- talk to someone
- ask whether this solves the real emotion
- use your accountability buddy (from Chapter 16)
- keep your goals visible

Awareness turns emotional spending into emotional intelligence.

BNPL: BUY NOW, PAY LATER = PAY LATER, PAY MORE

Afterpay, Zip, Klarna... all of the "Buy Now, Pay Later" services look helpful and feel convenient. But here's the reality:

Missed payment → fee
Fee → more pressure
Pressure → avoidance
Avoidance → more fees

BNPL is borrowing from Future You. And Future You is relying on Current You to take care of them! Start to create opinions for your future self now. And use BNPL *only* if you already have the money set aside.

DEBIT VS. CREDIT: THE SIMPLE RULE

Debit = your money
Credit = someone else's money, with strings attached

If you want to keep life simple, choose debit.

Credit is for later. Much later. When you understand exactly how it works.

SMART TIP

Give every dollar a job. Dollars with a job stick around. Dollars without one disappear.

RESEARCH RULE: 2 MINUTES = BIG SAVINGS

Online shopping makes everything feel urgent. But pausing to research almost always saves you money. Search for:

- cheaper sellers
- better reviews
- second-hand options
- bundles
- discount codes

Money saved is money you can use for something you care about.

It's incredibly easy to tap on an Instagram ad and buy something immediately, especially when the algorithms have been haunting you for days. They're very patient, so your wallet needs to be, too.

But those ads are designed to make the item feel urgent and exclusive, not necessarily affordable.

A quick search can change everything. Often, the same product is available elsewhere for a lot less. Maybe you can even find a secondhand version on Marketplace or Gumtree, that's a fraction of the new price. Or even discounted new options on Amazon or eBay. Taking a moment to compare options can lead to better quality, better reviews, and more trustworthy sellers. And comparison sites like Zyft can help you see what other stores charge in seconds and run the research for you.

And here's the best part: Every dollar you don't overspend becomes a dollar that can go towards your savings, your goals, or your future.

Research doesn't kill the fun of buying, it makes it cheaper, smarter, and more satisfying. How good does it feel to bag a bargain?

HEALTHY SPENDING HABITS

You enjoy your life.
You buy things that matter.
You skip things that don't.
You save without hating it.
You spend without guilt.
You feel calm.
You feel in control.
You feel proud of your choices. That feeling lasts longer than most impulse buys.

This is smart spending.

MINDFUL SPENDING

Being smart with money isn't only about finding the cheapest option, it involves making choices that line up with your values. Discount sites like Temu or SHEIN can feel like a win ("Why pay more?"), but it's worth pausing to ask: *What am I supporting?*

Some ultra-cheap products are linked to poor working conditions, environmental damage, or fast-fashion waste. The same goes for beauty products. If you care about animals, buying from a brand that still tests on them might clash with what you believe in.

Mindful spending means doing a little research, choosing brands you feel good about, and remembering that the "cheapest now" option might cost more in other ways. Vote with your money—where you spend it says something.

SMART TIP

Spend with intention, not impulse.

YOUR EMERGENCY BUFFER (YOUR FINANCIAL SEATBELT)

Life happens. Phones crack. Pets get sick. Cars break down. And unexpected costs pop up.

Having a money buffer turns chaos into inconvenience. Kind of like a seatbelt, it can feel boring and necessary... until you really need it.

Start small and build your buffer gradually. A simple approach is to aim for milestones such as $250, then $500, then $1,000.

You do not need to reach the full amount immediately. The goal is to build the habit of setting money aside so that unexpected expenses do not become emergencies. Slow and steady progress matters more than speed. Even small amounts saved consistently can create a helpful safety cushion over time.

Under the surface, this approach borrows from behavioural science. Large goals often overwhelm people, but small visible milestones keep motivation alive. Each step signals progress, and progress is one of the most powerful drivers of human behaviour. Over time those modest numbers quietly transform into real financial resilience.

SMART SHORTCUT

Comparison Sites Worth Checking Before You Buy

Before tapping "Buy Now," take sixty seconds to compare prices. It's amazing how often the exact same item is cheaper somewhere else—and those savings can go straight into your goals.

Here are a few Australian-friendly options:

- **Zyft:** *AI-powered search that scans tens of thousands of Aussie retailers instantly.*
- **PriceMe:** *Quick price comparisons on almost any product category.*
- **Getprice:** *Helps you find the best deal across a huge range of online stores.*
- **staticICE:** *Great for tech, gadgets and electronics at the lowest available price.*
- **ShopBot:** *Another broad comparison tool useful for everyday retail items.*

A tiny bit of research can save you a surprising amount, and make every purchase feel like a small win for Future You.

SMART TIP

Every dollar you save on the purchase is a dollar you can redirect towards something that matters to you. Spend with intention, not impulse. Spend on purpose, not pressure.

YOU DON'T NEED TO CUT EVERYTHING

Smart spending isn't restriction or saying "no" to everything. It's clarity. You don't have to give up:

- coffee, or even smashed avo on toast
- fashion
- eating out
- concerts
- small luxuries
- experiences that matter

You simply separate what you genuinely care about from what doesn't add value to your life. When you cut the noise, you can fund the things that truly support your life.

WHAT'S NEXT?

Now that you understand how spending works, it's time for the other side of the equation: **SMART Saving: Why It Matters More Than You Think.**

CHAPTER 5

SMART SAVING

"Do something today that your future self will thank you for."

—Sean Patrick Flanery

SMART Saving: Why It Matters More Than You Think

> *"Saving is not about having more money. It is about having more choices."*

Saving often gets painted as the "boring" part of money. But rather than viewing it as restriction, it's helpful to see it as *freedom in slow motion*.

Saving gives you:

- breathing room
- options
- flexibility
- security
- confidence
- choice.

The priority here is to give Future You a life that feels lighter, calmer, and kinder. Future You can start to have strong opinions about this. When you build the habit of saving, you're building far more than a bank balance, you're building confidence, control, and a future you can feel proud of.

Let's make saving simple, achievable, and surprisingly satisfying.

IT'S NOT ABOUT BEING PERFECT

When you have savings, life feels different:

- A bill doesn't ruin your week.

- A mistake doesn't become a crisis.
- A broken phone becomes an inconvenience, not a meltdown
- You can say yes to opportunities instead of watching them pass by.

Saving is not deprivation, it's preparation. And preparation is deeply underrated because it is self-respect in financial form.

SAVINGS = SECURITY, FREEDOM, FLEXIBILITY

When you have savings, you can make decisions based on what's right for you, not what your bank account demands.

Saving gives you:

- the ability to walk away from situations you've outgrown
- breathing room during stressful moments
- confidence that you can handle life's curveballs
- the power to take up opportunities when they appear

Saving isn't about hoarding money. It's about not panicking when life throws curveballs our way. Savings creates stability so you can move through life with more ease.

THE PAY-YOURSELF-FIRST MAGIC

There are two types of people: those who save what's left, and those who save first, then spend the rest. Category two wins every time.

Pay-yourself-first means moving a small amount into savings *as soon as* money hits your account. It can be tiny: $2, $5, $10,

$20. Small amounts saved consistently build confidence faster than large amounts saved rarely.

Future You will never complain about money you put aside. Never. Ever. Not once.

HOW MUCH SHOULD YOU SAVE?

Here's a simple guideline: Save 10–20% of any money that comes in.

If you get $50 from a shift:

- $5–$10 goes straight into savings
- The rest is yours to allocate

If 10% feels too much, start with 5%. Starting small still counts.

If 20% feels easy, go higher.

Saving is just like fitness—consistency matters more than scale and small, repeatable actions create big results.

> **SMART TIP**
>
> *Saving small amounts consistently beats saving big amounts randomly.*

BUCKET MINDSET: GIVE MONEY PURPOSE

Saving becomes easier when your money has a clear job.

Buckets create clarity without effort. And clarity makes good decisions much easier.

SPEND—Your Life Right Now Bucket

This is for living your life now: food, outings, fun, experiences, everyday costs. Spending is part of a healthy financial life.

SAVE—Your Stability Bucket

This is your buffer, your safety net, your short-term goals. It's what softens life's surprises.

GROW—Your Future Bucket

This is long-term money: investing, building wealth, creating options for Future You. You'll explore this more in Chapter 8.

GIVE—Your Impact Bucket

This one gets overlooked in most budgeting systems. It isn't necessary but it can be one of the most meaningful because this is about helping someone in need, gifts, or community support.

1. SPEND—YOUR LIFE RIGHT NOW BUCKET

Spending money is part of a healthy financial life. It's where joy, connection and everyday life happen.

Intentional spending gives you more joy than accidental spending. This bucket covers things that make your life run smoothly. It includes:

- food, eating out
- transport
- outings
- small purchases
- hobbies
- fun
- daily essentials, like board

Healthy spending isn't about restriction; it's about intention. Impulsive spending might give you the instant dopamine hit, but it's rarely satisfying for long.

LUCA'S REAL-LIFE EXAMPLE:

Luca used to buy takeaway lunches at work. Once he realised most of his spending bucket was disappearing, he swapped to prepared lunches and used the savings for a weekly dinner with friends, which was far more meaningful.

Same money. More joy. That's the power of intentional spending.

2. SAVE—YOUR STABILITY BUCKET

Your Save bucket is your safety net. It reduces stress, immediately.

It's for:

- emergencies
- unexpected bills
- small upgrades or replacements
- future events or short-term goals
- repairs
- surprise costs

An emergency buffer doesn't look glamorous, but it feels incredible. It means life can wobble without knocking you over. That feeling is worth way more than it sounds.

ZARA'S REAL-LIFE EXAMPLE:

Zara lost her laptop charger during exam week. Because she had a small emergency buffer, she was able to replace it the same day. A quick online search and overnight delivery. No panic, no borrowing, no stress.

One tiny moment, but a huge difference.

Saving doesn't just protect your finances; it protects your peace. A tiny buffer can give you a huge amount of relief and calm, which can be another massively underrated financial benefit.

3. GROW—YOUR FUTURE BUCKET

Your long-term bucket quietly builds to take care of Future You.

It covers:

- investing
- long-term saving

- wealth-building
- future goals (holidays, cars, moving out)
- anything that helps Future You live well

The Grow bucket rewards patience. This is where compound interest works its magic, and where small, consistent contributions create a life of choice and freedom.

It grows slowly at first, painfully slowly, but then dramatically over time. This is normal. Sadly, impatience doesn't speed it up.

NOAH'S REAL-LIFE EXAMPLE:

Noah started putting $20 a week into a long-term savings account. It didn't feel like much at the time, but after a year, he had over $1,000—enough to start a simple, low-fee index fund. He called it his "Future Fund."

That tiny habit completely changed the way he thought about money.

4. GIVE—YOUR KINDNESS BUCKET

Your Give bucket doesn't need to be big to make a big difference. It's not about donating large amounts, it's about having the capacity to help when something matters to you.

It might support:

- a cause
- a fundraiser
- a friend in crisis
- a community project

- a moment of kindness
- an unexpected need

BAXTER'S REAL-LIFE EXAMPLE:

When a neighbour's dog, Baxter, needed emergency surgery after an accident, the neighbourhood chipped in. Some gave $5, others $25. Together, they helped cover the bill.

Small amounts. Big impact.

That's true for money, and for kindness.

Giving creates connection and reminds you that money can do good, even in small doses. And if you can't afford to give monetarily, the greatest gift you can share is your time.

Why the Give Bucket Matters

Giving, even quietly, even occasionally, does something powerful. It:

- strengthens community
- builds gratitude
- connects you to something bigger than yourself
- turns money into impact, not pressure
- reminds you that generosity isn't about wealth, it's about intention

And here's the beautiful part: The more intentional your financial life becomes, the easier it is to be generous without stress.

The Give bucket lets you help without hurting yourself. Generosity feels very different when it's planned. It turns emotional moments into meaningful action and anchors your financial plan in compassion, rather than just calculation.

As a bonus, if you give money to a favourite charity that has DGR (Deductible Gift Recipient) status, you don't even pay tax on that money. It's completely tax deductible, which can help you score a bigger tax return.

TURNING GOALS INTO NUMBERS

A dream becomes achievable once you know the cost, deadline, and weekly amount required.

For example: A trip to Bali costs $5,000. If you plan twelve months in advance, you need to save $96 per week to achieve your goal. This dream is way more manageable when it's broken down early.

Numbers are information. And information makes decisions easier because they show you whether to adjust the amount, the plan, or the timeline. Once you know the real cost and the timeline, the path becomes obvious. And you can choose to either adjust the deadline, adjust the amount, or adjust the plan.

Saving is less about saying "no," and more about choosing how and when you say "yes."

EMMA'S SHOES-REAL LIFE EXAMPLE

Emma saved for months for a pair of expensive heels. When she finally bought them, she felt incredible—for three hours.

Then they hurt. They didn't match anything. And they couldn't be worn in the rain. So she sold them for half the price.

Saving wasn't the problem, but spending without a plan was.

Your buckets protect you from this.

SMART TIP

Saving is self-respect in weekly form.

THE POWER OF MOMENTUM

Once you start saving with intention, momentum builds.

You see progress.
Your account grows.
Your confidence grows with it.

It turns: $5 saved → $20 saved → "I can do this" → "Future Me will thank me"

Saving is more habit than maths. Once the habit forms, it develops its own rhythm.

SMART TIP

Saving isn't sacrifice, it's strategy and self-respect in weekly form.

EMERGENCY BUFFERS: YOUR FIRST PRIORITY

Life happens. Phones fall. Cars break. Pets get sick. An emergency buffer absorbs chaos and turns disasters into annoyances.

Start small: $250 → $500 → $1,000. Then build it, brick by brick.

Future You will treasure this bucket.

SHORT-TERM SAVING

Anything you can save for within twelve months is a short-term goal. For example:

- concerts
- laptops
- road trips
- new tech
- holidays
- formal outfits

Steps:

- Name the goal
- Know the cost
- Set the deadline
- Divide cost by weeks
- Automate transfers

Most banking apps can do this for you.

SMART TIP

If your savings are mixed with your spending money, they're not savings—they're snacks waiting to happen.

AUTOMATIC SAVING (YOUR SECRET WEAPON)

If saving relies on willpower, life usually wins.

If saving is automated, you win.

Here are a few simple ways to make saving happen automatically:

- Round up tools
- The 50/50 rule (half for now, half for later)
- Digital pockets or savings buckets
- The 24 hour rule before non-essential purchases

Automation = habits built while you sleep. This is possibly the most efficient use of tech.

SAVING WITH FRIENDS (SURPRISINGLY FUN)

Do you want to save for something together? Try:

- no-spend weekends
- stay-in nights
- group cooking
- thrifting
- carpooling
- shared challenges

You don't have to save by yourself; it can be a team sport—with fewer injuries and better snacks!

WHEN SAVING FEELS HARD

It's perfectly normal for some weeks to feel impossible and for some months to feel heavy. When things get tricky, return to your plan when you can. A pause isn't failure, it's part of being human. You can restart anytime.

WHY STARTING EARLY IS A SUPERPOWER

Most adults wish they'd learned how to save earlier in their lives. The earlier you start, the easier it becomes to:

- move out
- buy your first car
- travel
- build investments
- handle emergencies
- stay independent

Saving early gives Future You choices—big ones. And choices feel a LOT better than pressure.

ACTIVITY: CREATE YOUR BUCKET SYSTEM

Take fifteen minutes and set this up:

Start by creating three simple categories for your money: *Spend*, *Save*, and *Grow*. If you like the idea of giving, you can add a fourth category called *Give*.

You can organise this in whatever way works for you. Some people use separate bank accounts, while others create sub accounts or savings "buckets" within their banking app. The goal is simply to give each dollar a clear purpose so your money is organised rather than mixed together.

Decide what goes into each bucket each time you get money.

Write down one short term goal and one long term goal that your Save and Grow buckets will support. For example, a short term goal might be saving for a concert, new headphones, or a school trip. A long term goal might be a car, travel, or future study.

SPEND	SAVE	GROW

Track your progress for two weeks and check how it feels.

You'll be surprised how quickly you feel more in control.

WHAT'S NEXT?

By now, you've learned how to earn, spend, save and make intentional choices with your money. So naturally, the next curiosity pops up: *Can my money start to work for me?*

Chapter 6—SMART Micro-Investing: Start Small, Learn Fast, Grow Wisely is where investing stops feeling intimidating and starts to feel possible. It's about starting small, learning safely, and understanding how investing works before the stakes get big.

No pressure. No "get rich quick" nonsense. No pretending spare change makes you Warren Buffett, one of the most successful investors in the world. Just a smart, low-stress way to build confidence, form good habits, and learn what really matters before moving on to bigger investing decisions.

CHAPTER 6

SMART MICRO INVESTING

"An investment in knowledge pays the best interest."

—Benjamin Franklin

SMART Micro-Investing: Start Small, Learn Fast, Grow Wisely

> *"You don't need a lot of money to start. You just need to start smart."*

Micro-investing feels like the perfect beginning—and for many teens, it is. Doing this lets you invest tiny amounts, sometimes even spare change, and gives you a simple way to see how the market moves. No pressure. No jargon. No big decisions. Just learning by doing.

Think of it as a test drive rather than a lifetime commitment. But starting small doesn't mean staying small forever. Everyone must start somewhere.

Micro-investing teaches you the *habits* that make a great investor: showing up consistently, thinking long-term, and not panicking when your balance goes up or down. It's a stepping stone, not a full investing strategy; it's useful, but not where you'll permanently set up camp.

And to use it well, you need to understand how the platforms work, what they cost, and when it's time to graduate to something more powerful.

This chapter helps you understand the good, the convenient, and the slightly sneaky parts of micro-investing so you can choose wisely and build confidence without wasting money on fees.

Here's a micro chapter for a micro cause.

SMART TIP

Easy doesn't always mean cheaper. Micro-investing apps look friendly and simple, but simplicity often comes with higher fees. Before signing up, check what you're paying and whether the platform supports the kind of future you want. Friendly apps still charge real money.

REAL TALK

Micro-investing can make you feel like you're investing seriously—even when you're only building tiny balances. That's okay. Feeling confident is part of the journey. Confidence is good. But blind confidence is expensive. Confidence grows faster when you understand the costs and know when to level up.

WHO MICRO-INVESTING IS GOOD FOR

Micro-investing is great when you:

- want to learn how investing works
- want to build confidence slowly
- start with very small amounts
- prefer simple apps and don't want to make big choices yet
- want to practice consistent saving habits
- want to invest but feel intimidated by ETFs or brokerage platforms

It's basically "training wheels investing." Safe. Simple. Low pressure. Great for balance, not built for speed.

> ⚠ **WARNING**
>
> **When Micro-Investing Isn't a Good Fit**
>
> *Micro-investing isn't ideal when:*
> - *Your balance is extremely small*
> - *The monthly fee is a huge percentage of your investment*
> - *You're picking portfolios because they sound fun, not because you understand them*
> - *You rely on roundups instead of intentional saving*
> - *You think micro-investing is the whole strategy*
>
> *Convenience is great. Confusion is costly.*

EASY ENTRY, BUT KNOW THE FINE PRINT

Micro-investing apps like Raiz, Spaceship, Sharesies, and Pearler Micro make it simple to start with tiny amounts. They're user-friendly and designed to help beginners feel comfortable.

But simple doesn't always mean cheaper. It could be like buying the cheapest headphones online and discovering the sound is terrible and they break a week later.

Some apps charge *monthly subscription fees* which can swallow your returns if your balance is small. Others offer portfolios that sound exciting but don't align with long-term investing best practice.

SMART TIP

Look beyond the app design. Before using a micro-investing platform, check:

- *What are the fees? (Even $3.50 a month is a big percentage if you only have $50 invested.)*
- *What am I actually investing in?*
- *Does this support my goals, or is it just convenient?*

Convenience fades. Fees stick around.

COMPARING PLATFORMS[1]

	Raiz	Spaceship	Sharesies	Pearler Micro (Kids)
MINIMUM INVESTMENT:	Roundups or lump sums	$0 minimum	Very small amounts	Very small amounts
FEES:	Monthly fee + % fee on larger balances	Percentage-based fee after first $100	Percentage-based	Low, flat subscription
WHAT YOU SHOULD KNOW:	Fun to start, but monthly fees can overwhelm small balances. Check portfolios carefully.	App is simple and clean; long-term performance and fees matter more than design.	Allows fractional shares—great for learning. Requires an adult for custodial accounts.	Auto-invest options are very beginner-friendly. Be aware of total yearly cost.

1 **Note:** Under 18's always need a parent or guardian to open and supervise these accounts.

SMART MOVE

Move to Your Long-Term Strategy

Here's the easy version: Graduate when your balance reaches $1,000–$3,000, and a full platform becomes cheaper and better long-term. Many people miss the moment when you need to move from staying small to being ready to grow. More specifically:

Raiz

Graduate at $1,000–$2,000
Flat fees are too expensive on tiny balances.

Spaceship

Graduate at $2,000–$3,000
Percentage fees are okay early, but ETFs are cheaper long-term.

Sharesies

Graduate around $1,000–$2,000
Great for beginners but brokerage becomes cheaper elsewhere.

Pearler Micro

Graduate at $3,000+
Flat subscription fees become better value as balances grow.

SMART TIP

Micro-investing makes sense when your balance is small. It stops making sense when your fees become bigger than your growth.

If the cost feels big compared to your balance → time to level up.

If the cost feels tiny compared to your balance → you're fine to stay a little longer. Just don't forget to reassess. Staying on autopilot isn't a strategy.

Micro-investing is a great way to start small, learn slowly, and build confidence without feeling overwhelmed. But once you understand the basics and your balance begins to grow, it's time to take the next step: learning how *real* investing works. That's where SMART Investing comes in—because it helps you choose investments intentionally, avoid hype, understand risk properly, and build wealth over time. From there, we step into SMART Super, one of the most powerful wealth tools you'll ever have, and then into SMART Fees, where you'll learn how tiny costs can shape your long-term financial future. You're building a system now, and every chapter strengthens your foundation.

REAL TALK

Micro-investing is like training wheels. They help you start. But eventually taking them off makes the ride smoother, cheaper, and more empowering.

WHAT'S NEXT?

Micro-investing is a great place to start because it lets you learn, build confidence, and see how markets move without risking much. But at some point, starting small turns into thinking bigger.

Chapter 7—SMART Investing: Grow Your Money Without Stress is where you move beyond training wheels and understand *why* you invest, how to choose investments intentionally, and how to grow money over time without chasing hype or panicking when markets wobble.

No shortcuts.
No hot tips.
No guessing.

Just calm, long-term investing that actually works.

CHAPTER 7

SMART INVESTING

"The stock market is a device for transferring money from the impatient to the patient."

—Warren Buffett

SMART Investing: Grow Your Money Without Stress

> *"The real secret to investing isn't brilliance. It's starting early and staying steady."*

Investing often sounds big and intimidating, but here's the secret: You don't need to be rich, gifted or a maths genius. You need three things, and a crystal ball ain't one of them!

- a bit of knowledge
- a bit of patience
- a simple plan

Investing is simply putting money somewhere to grow over time.

That's it. And ideally more exciting than stashing cash in your sock drawer.

Earning money feels empowering, and investing can feel like discovering a cheat code. Except it's not cheating, it's just maths, time, and calm decisions. Feeling calm may be optional to start with, but it will improve with practice.

Investing is about understanding one powerful idea: *Money can work for you while you sleep.* This is handy when you're busy living your best life.

Once you know how to do that safely, you unlock options that most people don't discover until much later in life. Let's keep it simple, calm, and surprisingly enjoyable.

WHY INVEST AT ALL?

Saving is great. It gives you:

- safety
- stability
- breathing room

But saving has a limit. While it keeps you safe, it doesn't get you ahead.

Money sitting in a bank grows *very* slowly because interest rates are usually low. Investing is how you *give your money a job*. Over time, investing can help you:

- grow wealth
- reach big goals sooner
- beat inflation
- support the life you want
- give Future You more choices
- build financial confidence

Investing is long-term kindness to yourself.

TWO MYTHS ABOUT INVESTING

MYTH 1: "I need a lot of money to start."

Not true. Many platforms let you invest from $5, $10, or $20.

The amount doesn't matter. The habit does. Habits quietly beat big intentions every time.

MYTH 2: "It's too risky for me."

It's only risky when you don't understand it. Once you know the basics, investing becomes calm and predictable.

Knowledge reduces fear. And fear is what usually makes investing feel scarier than it needs to be.

WHAT INVESTING ACTUALLY IS

Investing is using money today to buy something that grows in value, or earns income, or both. It's not mystical, or just for "finance people." And it's definitely not reserved for the guys in suits on TV. You might invest in:

- Shares–tiny slices of companies
- ETFs – baskets of shares you buy in one go
- Managed funds
- Property
- Bonds
- Superannuation (yes, this is investing too)
- Businesses
- Skills that increase your earning power

Good investing isn't about picking one magic winner, it's about *consistency* and *long-term thinking*.

To keep it simple, think of three main places money can grow:

- **Businesses (Shares/Stocks):** You own a tiny slice of a company. If the company grows and makes money, your slice becomes more valuable.
- **Property (Real Estate):** You can invest directly (buy a property) or indirectly (through property funds).

- **Mixed Options (Managed Funds / ETFs):** These are bundles of investments you buy in one go—like a grazing board instead of picking every single item yourself.

Many people start here because it's simple and less stressful. *Simple* ages better than *clever*.

THE ONLY INVESTING FORMULA YOU NEED

This isn't a trick. Time + Consistency = Growth

You don't need to pick the perfect investment.
You don't need to be a genius.
You don't need to "time the market."

You just need to start, keep going, and stay calm.

Messy starts are still starts. Compounding will do most of the heavy lifting.

SMART TIP

Time in the market beats trying to "time" the market.

THE MAGIC OF COMPOUNDING

Compounding is when: your money earns money → then *that* money earns money → then *that* money also earns money → and the snowball keeps rolling.

Time is the secret ingredient.

- Start early? Even small amounts can grow surprisingly large.
- Start later? Still worth it—but early years are priceless.

Compounding is the closest thing money has to a superpower. Unfortunately, it only works if you give it time.

THE MONEY SNOWBALL

Two friends invest:

- Alex invests $20 a week from age 20 to 30, then stops.
- Jordan starts at age 30, invests $20 a week, and keeps going for 35 years.

Alex only invests for 10 years. Jordan invests for 35.

Who ends up with more? **Alex.** Because compounding rewards early starters, not just hard workers.

Another example:

If you invest $25 a week from age 16 to 30 (14 years), earning an average of 8% per year, you could end up with around $32,000.

Keep going to age 40? You could end up with closer to $86,000.

Keep going to age 50? Over $200,000.

Time is your superpower. Small, early, consistent steps do more than you may think.

RISK: THE PART EVERYONE OVERREACTS TO

Risk isn't "good" or "bad." It simply means how much the value of your investment changes over time.

- Higher risk = bigger ups and downs
- Lower risk = smaller ups and downs

You don't need to avoid risk, but you do need to choose the *right level* of risk for your goals, timeframe, and personality.

The longer you stay invested, the smoother the ride tends to feel.

Some examples:

- **Low risk:** cash, savings accounts, term deposits, government bonds
- **Medium risk:** diversified funds, broad ETFs
- **Higher risk:** individual shares, property, crypto, speculative "get rich quick" stuff

Higher risk *can* mean higher returns, but also bigger bumps along the way.

The key is matching your personality and your goals and your timeframe. If something keeps you awake at night, it's too risky *for you.* Sleeping well is another underrated financial skill. If your investment keeps you up at night, it's probably a little too exciting.

There are questionnaires that help you work out whether your risk style is:

- Conservative
- Balanced
- Growth
- Aggressive

You might choose safer options for shorter-term goals (car, travel), and higher growth options for long-term goals (like super).

REASONS FOR INVESTING

Most investors are chasing one (or a mixture) of three things:

- **Income:** Regular payments like interest or dividends. Good for people who want steady, predictable returns.
- **Growth:** Buying something you hope will be worth more later. This is where things like property, shares and crypto often sit. Higher potential reward, but more volatility.
- **Blended / Balanced:** A mix of income and growth, so you get some stability and some long-term upside.

You don't have to pick just one forever and your mix can change as your life changes. Flexibility is a feature, not a flaw.

> **SMART TIP**
>
> *If an investment promises massive returns with no risk, it's lying to you.*

DIVERSIFICATION: BORING BUT BRILLIANT

Diversification just means *don't put everything in one place*. If you have:

- one shoe and lose it → you're barefoot
- ten pairs and lose one → you're fine

Investing is the same. If all your money is in one company and it fails, you're in trouble. But if your money is spread across many companies, industries and countries, one bad day doesn't destroy your future.

Diversified investments:

- smooth out the bumps
- reduce the impact of any single disaster
- make it easier to stay calm when news headlines get dramatic

That's why a lot of new investors start with ETFs or managed funds. "Boring" investing can be surprisingly effective.

SHARES: OWNING TINY PIECES OF BIG THINGS

Buying a share means you own a *fraction* of a company. If the company grows and makes profit over time, your slice becomes more valuable. People imagine the share market as chaos and shouting (thanks, Hollywood), but it's really:

- companies trying to grow
- people investing for their future
- prices moving based on expectations and news

Far less shouting, and far more patience.

Long term, markets tend to grow. Short term, they wobble. That wobble is called *volatility*. And the media loves to dramatise it.

You might recognise some big Australian companies, such as:

- Commonwealth Bank (CBA)
- BHP Group (BHP)
- Woolworths (WOW)
- Telstra (TLS)
- (Formerly) Afterpay (APT) before its acquisition

You don't need to learn about every company. That's where *managed funds* come in.

MANAGED FUNDS AND ETFS: EASY MODE

Managed funds and Exchange-Traded Funds (ETFs) let you buy lots of companies in one go. Think of them as:

- a *playlist,* instead of choosing every song
- a *grazing board,* instead of picking every item
- a *highlights reel,* instead of watching every episode

They save time, spread risk, and give you instant diversification

ETFs are popular worldwide because they're:

- low cost
- diversified
- designed for long-term growth
- fairly hands-off

Most new investors keep it simple and choose:

- a broad Australian share fund
- a broad international share fund
- or a low-cost index or balanced fund

Low cost + diversified + long term = calm investing.

A QUICK EXAMPLE:

VAS (Vanguard Australian Shares Index ETF) invests across the S&P/ASX 300: roughly the top 300 companies in Australia.

IOO (iShares Global 100) invests in around 100 of the largest companies in the world, including big global names.

None of these are recommendations, they are simply examples of how ETFs can cover a lot in one go. Choosing an ETF over a managed fund dramatically reduces decision fatigue.

Thematic ETFs

Thematic ETFs let you invest in a big idea rather than a single company. Themes might include:

- robotics and/or AI
- clean energy and renewables
- cybersecurity
- space tech

One purchase = a basket of companies connected to that theme.

They're exciting, but can cause sleepless nights because they:

- count as growth investments
- can rise quickly when the theme is popular
- can fall just as fast when interest cools

They work best if you understand the theme, accept the risk, and treat them as a *smaller* part of a broader plan. Again, examples like *ROBO* (a robotics ETF) show how you can spread your bet across many companies instead of just one. But they're still growth focused and can be bumpy.

> **REAL TALK**
>
> *Crypto is exciting, unpredictable, and often over-hyped online. It's also completely different from long-term investing. We'll cover the risks and realities in a dedicated chapter later, so you can explore it safely and with clear eyes. Calm curiosity beats hype every time.*

WHAT YOU ACTUALLY NEED TO START INVESTING

You don't need a finance degree, but you do need:

- a bank account
- ID
- a small amount of money
- a platform (micro-investing app *or* low-fee investment account)
- patience

You learn by doing. Slowly, safely, and with small amounts at first. This is how you will build your confidence.

HOW TO START INVESTING (WITHOUT STRESS)

Most people begin by:

- opening a micro-investing app or low-fee investment platform
- choosing a simple, diversified ETF or fund

- investing small amounts regularly
- ignoring the noise and short-term drama
- letting time do its thing

The most important step is simply *starting*. Perfect decisions are overrated.

A REAL-LIFE SNAPSHOT: THE $10 HABIT

Investing $10 a week at a modest return could grow into:

- around $2,000 in a few years
- around $10,000 in your twenties or thirties
- tens of thousands over decades
- far more if you increase contributions later

Small actions → big results, especially when they're "boring" enough to stick with.

HOW MUCH SHOULD YOU INVEST?

There's no perfect number, but as a simple guideline: *Start with whatever feels comfortable.*

$5 a week
$10 a week
$25 a week

The point is the habit because the habit builds confidence, and confidence builds wealth and makes everything easier.

Putting money into savings first, then investing in sensible chunks, can also help you save on fees like brokerage. If a platform charges $20 to buy an ETF:

- Investing $500 means $480 invested (4% gone in fees).
- Investing $1,000 means $980 invested (2% in fees).

Some platforms also charge ongoing fees—we'll unpack that properly in the **SMART Fees** chapter.

ACTIVITY: YOUR FIRST GROWTH PLAN

This isn't a commitment, it's a vision exercise. You're allowed to change your mind as you learn. Clarity always comes before confidence.

Write down:

- one long-term goal (5+ years)
- one investment type you're curious about
- one small amount you could invest regularly
- what you hope Future You gains from it

LOW-COST AUSTRALIAN BROKERS TO RESEARCH

When you're ready to move beyond micro-investing, it's worth comparing low-cost brokers. Research always beats rushing, especially with money. Here are a few options to research in your own time (not recommendations, just starting points):

- CommSec Pocket
- Linked to Commonwealth Bank
- Invest in themed ETFs from relatively low amounts
- Simple fee structure and beginner friendly app
- Vanguard Personal Investor
- Direct access to index funds and ETFs
- Known globally for low fees and long-term focus
- Sharesies (Australia)
- Fractional investing so you can buy small portions of shares
- Clear and simple fee structure
- Pearler / Pearler Kids
- Flat-fee approach with a strong focus on long-term investing
- Automation tools to build investing habits
- SelfWealth
- Flat-fee brokerage regardless of trade size
- Often used by ETF-focussed investors

Note: Investors under 18 generally need a parent or guardian involved to open and manage an account.

> **SMART TIP**
>
> *Low fees help your investments grow faster over time. A small difference in fees today can turn into a big difference in your future balance. Part of being a SMART investor is researching not just the platform you like... but the true cost of using it.*

REAL TALK

No broker lets under-18s open accounts fully on their own. You always need a parent or guardian involved. Look at this as protection. It's training, with supervision, and it's a great chance to start healthy money conversations at home.

WHAT'S NEXT?

You now understand how money can grow calmly, steadily, and with intention. But growing money is only half the picture.

For most people, the largest investment they'll ever have isn't something they choose. It's superannuation. And yet it's also the one most people understand the least.

In the next chapter, **SMART Super: Your Future Self's Secret Weapon**, you'll learn:

- what super actually is (in plain English)
- why it's one of the most powerful long-term wealth tools available
- how small choices now can make a big difference later
- how to avoid common mistakes that erode your balance
- how to feel confident and clear about something that runs quietly in the background of your life

I understand that when you're young, retirement is a REALLY, REALLY long time away. And super isn't exciting. But that's exactly why it works!

When you understand superannuation early, it becomes one of the easiest ways to let money grow while you focus on living your life.

So let's demystify it.

CHAPTER 8

SMART SUPER

"Small daily improvements over time lead to stunning results."

—Robin Sharma

SMART Super: Your Future Self's Secret Weapon

> *"The earlier you start building super, the harder your money works while you get on with living your life."*

Superannuation is one of those things most people ignore until much later in life... and then wish they hadn't. You don't need to obsess over it. You don't need to log in every week. And you definitely don't need to understand every line of legislation.

But you do need to know how super works, why it matters, and how to set it up well. Once you do, your super will grow quietly in the background while you get on with living your life.

Think of it as Future You's long-term financial safety net.

WHAT SUPER ACTUALLY IS

Superannuation is a long-term investment account designed to support you later in life when you don't (or can't) work anymore. Again, not good, not bad, It's just a tool; a *very* long-term tool. A slow cooker, not a microwave.

Every time you work, your employer must pay a percentage of your earnings, the *Super Guarantee*, into your super fund. It doesn't come out of your pay, it's on top of what you earn.

You earn money for now. Your super earns money for later. It's a simple idea with enormous long-term impact.

WHY SUPER GROWS SO MUCH OVER TIME

1. Compounding

- Your super gets invested
- It earns returns
- Those returns earn returns
- And the cycle repeats for decades

Snowball → rolling → growing → powerful. Very small at the start, but incredibly impressive later.

2. Consistent Contributions

Every time you're paid, more money goes into your super, even when you forget about it.

3. Time

Super has 40+ years to grow. You can't buy time. In the investment world, that's pure gold. Your future self is quietly cheering every dollar you put into super.

CHRIS' SUPER

Chris started working casually at Maccas while still in high school. She'll likely have thousands in super before she even finishes her teens. Fast-forward several decades, and those early contributions can grow into something seriously meaningful.

Super isn't exciting. But the results are. The more she puts aside now, the more Future Chris will thank her.

INVESTMENT OPTIONS (NO JARGON)

Most funds offer a few simple investment choices such as:

- Balanced
- Growth
- High Growth
- Conservative
- Ethical or Sustainable options

These names describe how the money is invested and how much risk the fund is taking. Growth options usually invest more in shares, while Conservative options hold more cash and fixed interest.

If you are early in your working life and have decades ahead, Growth or Balanced options often make sense because they allow more time for investments to grow.

Decades might sound like a long time, but that is exactly when time can work hardest for you.

There is no rush to change anything straight away. The default investment option in most super funds is usually designed to be a sensible starting point. As you learn more about investing over time, you may decide to explore other options.

Retail funds like Master Trusts and Wraps have more comprehensive options:

- Index Funds
- Actively Managed Funds
- Individual Shares
- ETF options

You don't need to understand everything at this stage. Simply knowing your choices exist helps you avoid some of the biggest mistakes.

INDEX FUNDS VS. DEFAULT FUNDS

Super funds usually invest your money using either:

- **Active options:** Human fund managers try to pick the best investments.
- **Index options:** Your money simply tracks the market automatically.

Index options often have a powerful advantage because they're usually much cheaper. Lower fees can mean tens, even hundreds, or thousands, of dollars more over your lifetime.

Small percentages get very powerful over time. A difference of just one or two percent in fees or returns may not seem important today, but over forty years it can dramatically change how much you end up with.

The strange magic here is compounding. Imagine two plants growing side by side. One grows just a little faster each year. For the first few years they look almost the same. Four decades later, one is a towering tree and the other is a shrub wondering what happened. Tiny percentages decide which one you become.

Default funds often use a mix of active and passive strategies. They're designed to be sensible and simple, but they can be more expensive than a pure index option.

> **SMART TIP**
>
> *Lower fees + long timeframes = stronger long-term outcomes.*

WHAT EXACTLY IS AN INDEX FUND?

An index fund tracks a list of companies rather than trying to beat it.

For example:

- **ASX 200:** Australia's top 200 companies
- **S&P 500:** 500 major US companies
- **Global indexes:** diversified worldwide investing

When the market rises, index funds rise. When markets fall, the index funds fall too. Over long periods, markets tend to grow. Index funds simply ride that trend cheaply.

WHY WARREN BUFFETT LOVES INDEX FUNDS

Warren Buffett, one of the most successful investors in history, says: "When trillions of dollars are managed by Wall Streeters charging high fees, it will usually be the managers who reap outsized profits, not the clients." His recommendation for most people is to: *Keep it simple. Use low-cost index funds. Don't overpay.* It's hard to argue with that.

INDEX OPTIONS INSIDE SUPER

Many Australian super funds offer:

- Indexed Balanced
- Indexed Growth

- Indexed High Growth
- Indexed Australian Shares
- Indexed International Shares

These options often have dramatically lower fees.

A rough example:

- **Default fund:** 0.7–1.3%
- **Index option:** 0.1–0.3%

Over 40+ years, that difference is massive. "Boring" wins again.

> **SMART TIP**
>
> *Super works best when you set it up well, check it occasionally, and then let time do the heavy lifting.*

CHOOSING A SUPER FUND (WITHOUT THE OVERWHELM)

A good super fund is simply:

- Low-fee
- Strong long-term performance (look at 8–10 years, not last year)
- Transparent (easy to see investments, fees, and insurance)
- Clear insurance options (you should understand what you're paying for)

Ignore glossy marketing. Focus on the substance. Super doesn't need to be exciting, it needs to work.

HELPFUL WEBSITES (INDEPENDENT AND RELIABLE)

- **MoneySmart (ASIC):** moneysmart.gov.au
- **ATO YourSuper Comparison:** ato.gov.au/YourSuper
- **Choice:** choice.com.au

Sites like Canstar, Finder, and RateCity are useful starting points but always cross-check with unbiased sources.

AVOIDING THE MULTIPLE ACCOUNTS TRAP

Working multiple jobs often leads to multiple super accounts. Multiple accounts = multiple sets of fees.

The ideal number of super accounts? *One*. Fewer accounts means fewer fees and less chaos.

> **SMART TIP**
>
> *Before consolidating your accounts, check the insurance attached to each as closing an account cancels insurance instantly.*

INSURANCE IN SUPER

Default super insurance used to be automatic for everyone, but rules changed to protect young workers from premium erosion.

Now:

- Most funds only turn on insurance automatically at 25+ with at least $6,000 in the account.
- Under 25s can still get insurance, but they must opt in.

Insurance in super can include:

- Life insurance
- Total & Permanent Disability (TPD)
- Income protection

For some young people, especially those without savings or family support, default TPD can be life changing.

Ask yourself:

- Do I have anyone relying on me?
- Would losing my ability to work ruin me financially?
- Do I have savings or backup?

For young workers, low premiums = valuable protection. You'll hope you never need it, but you'll be glad if you do.

BEFORE YOU COMBINE: CHECK YOUR INSURANCE

If you close a super account to roll into a new one, any insurance attached to it disappears immediately.

Super-based insurance can include:

- Life insurance
- TPD
- Income protection

Sometimes it's cheap and valuable. Sometimes it's unnecessary. The important part is knowing what you're losing.

Quick checklist:

- Log in to each super fund
- Open the Insurance section

- See what cover you have
- Decide if you want to keep or replace it
- Only consolidate once replacement cover is active

ARJUN'S SUPER

Arjun combined his super accounts to make things simpler. But he did not realise that one of the accounts included TPD insurance.

When the account was closed, the insurance was cancelled too. Later, when he tried to get the same cover again, he could not because of a health condition he had developed.

The lesson: Always check whether insurance is attached to a super account before closing or combining it.

CHECK YOUR EMPLOYER IS PAYING YOUR SUPER

It's more common than you think for employers to fall behind.

How to check:

- Log in to your super
- Look under Contributions
- Check SG (Super Guarantee) payments
- Compare dates with your pay cycle or pay slips

If something looks off, ask payroll politely. Most issues are simple mistakes and get fixed quickly.

Asking politely works more often than you might expect. As my old man always said, "You catch more flies with honey than vinegar!"

PAYDAY SUPER (A BIG WIN FOR WORKERS IN AUSTRALIA)

Australia is introducing *payday super*, meaning:

- Super is paid at the same time as wages
- Payments are more frequent
- Gaps are easier to spot
- Contributions compound sooner

This is a massive improvement for young workers. Faster contributions mean more time compounding can work its magic!

WHAT'S ACTUALLY INSIDE YOUR SUPER FUND

Super funds invest your money in things like:

- shares
- property
- infrastructure
- bonds
- cash
- diversified funds
- index funds

You choose an investment option and the fund handles the rest. If you don't choose, you'll be placed in a *Default* option, which is not always the cheapest. Make sure you set it up well, then let it run.

WHY SUPER MATTERS MORE THAN PEOPLE THINK

Super is not just about retirement. It is about creating options for your future. When you have options, your choices are driven by what you want to do, not what you have to do.

It's about the freedom to:

- work less, someday
- leave a job that drains you
- choose your own lifestyle
- avoid money stress later

Superannuation is Future You's best friend.

📒 ACTIVITY: YOUR SUPER SNAPSHOT

Take five minutes to:

- [ ] Log into your super
- [ ] Check your balance
- [ ] Check your investment option
- [ ] Look at your insurance
- [ ] Review the fees
- [ ] Ensure contributions are up to date
- [ ] Identify any duplicate accounts

It's the quickest financial habit with the biggest payoff.

WHAT'S NEXT?

Super grows over decades—quietly, consistently, and powerfully. But there's a hidden force that shapes that growth behind the scenes: the fees.

Fees might look tiny, but over 40+ years they can make an enormous difference to your final balance. Understanding fees is empowering. Once you know what they are and how they work, you can keep more of your money growing for your future rather than letting it leak away unnoticed.

In the next chapter, we'll break down:

- the types of fees you'll encounter
- how to compare them
- how they impact long-term returns
- and how to keep fees working *for* you, not against you

Next up: **SMART Fees: Understand Investment Costs**

Understanding fees is one of the fastest ways to become a more confident investor, without taking on more risk.

CHAPTER 9

SMART FEES

"Beware of little expenses; a small leak will sink a great ship."

—Benjamin Franklin

Smart Fees: Understand Investment Costs

> *"Fees compound just like investments do. The difference is they compound against you."*

When you invest, your money can earn returns and there are also small costs involved in keeping it invested. These are called fees. They aren't necessarily bad; they're simply the price of using investment platforms, funds, and professional managers. You're paying for the infrastructure and access to expertise.

Sadly, ignoring fees doesn't make them disappear. Understanding them helps you make smarter choices.

Fees are one of the most important things to understand when managing your money. They often look small and are sometimes hidden in the fine print, but over time they can make a big difference to how much you end up with.

In this chapter, you'll learn the common types of investment fees and what they mean in simple terms, so you can make informed decisions and ensure they work for you, not against you.

WHY FEES MATTER

When you invest, choose a super fund, or trade shares, you pay small ongoing costs. Fees are simply the cost of running the systems, people, technology, and funds behind the scenes. Fund managers, analysts, compliance teams, technology platforms, and custodians all play a role in keeping investments running smoothly, legally, and securely. Good funds don't operate on guesswork, they rely on research, systems, and oversight. But here's the part most people miss: *A tiny fee difference now can become a huge difference later.*

Small percentages can become surprisingly powerful over long periods of time, and just as they can work *for you* when investing, they'll work *against you* when left unchecked.

The goal isn't to avoid fees altogether. Don't freak out about them because paying fees is normal. The aim is to understand what you're paying for and make sure the cost matches the value.

Lower fees = more money left invested = more compounding for your future.

FOUR MAIN TYPES OF FEES

1. Admin Fees: Running Your Account

Admin fees pay for the cost of keeping your account open. This includes:

- online portals
- statements
- customer support
- security and systems

They can be:

- a small flat fee (e.g., $78 a year)
- a percentage of your balance
- a combination of both.

Admin fees are ongoing and don't depend on how often you trade or invest. Think of them as the cost of keeping the lights on.

2. Management Costs: Running the Investments

These are the costs of managing the actual fund your money sits in.

The fund uses professionals who:

- analyse markets
- choose investments
- balance risk
- do research
- maintain the fund

Management costs are taken out quietly in the background, which means you won't get a bill. But they will slightly reduce your return each year. Be aware that over time, "slightly" can add up too.

3. ICR: Indirect Cost Ratio

This is part of the management fee, and covers the internal expenses of running the fund, such as:

- research
- trading costs
- legal and regulatory requirements
- internal operations

The ICR is always shown as a percentage, such as 0.10% or 0.75%. Tiny numbers deserve your attention too.

SMART TIP

Compare ICRs when choosing funds. Lower ICRs help your money grow faster over time because less of your investment is being used to pay fund management costs. Lower fees may not sound exciting, but they mean more of your money stays invested and continues to grow.

4. Brokerage: The Cost to Buy or Sell

Whenever you trade shares or ETFs, your broker charges a *transaction fee*. This could be:

a flat amount (like $0–$10 per trade)

or

a percentage of your order

Some low-cost brokers now offer zero brokerage on certain products, but it's always important to read the fine print. Low brokerage doesn't automatically mean low overall fees.

Cheap entry can still mean expensive ownership.

REAL TALK

The more you trade, the more you pay. Long-term investors pay the least in fees because they buy, hold, and let the money grow.

Patience is surprisingly cost-effective.

WHAT DO FEES LOOK LIKE IN REAL LIFE?

Here's a simple example comparing two funds over 20 years:

	Low Fee Fund (0.20%)	High Fee Fund (1.00%)
Value after 20 years	$7,408	$6,099
Money lost to fees	≈ $182	≈ $1,491

The investments work the same.
The difference is entirely fees.
That extra $1,309 could have been yours.

Same investments, but very different outcomes.

SMART MOVE

Always check a fund's **Fee Breakdown** *before you join. If you don't understand the fee, ask. You're not supposed to know this stuff automatically. Learning to notice fees is already a win.*

HOW TO BE A SMART FEE CHECKER

A quick checklist you can use before choosing a fund or broker:

- Do they charge admin fees? If yes, how much?
- What is the management fee?
- What is the ICR? (a.k.a. management fee)
- Are there platform fees on top?
- What does brokerage cost?

- Is there a minimum investment?
- Does the cost reflect the value?

Value can matter more than hype.

If a fund charges a higher fee because it is actively managed, ask:

- "Do the long-term results justify it?"
- "Am I paying extra for something I don't need?"

FEES AREN'T THE ENEMY, JUST A FACTOR

You don't have to pick the lowest-fee option every time. The goal is to make informed decisions instead of accidental ones.

Accidental fees are expensive!

When you understand fees, you take control of one of the most important parts of your financial future.

WARNING

Don't Chase "Zero Fees" Without Reading the Fine Print

Some platforms remove one fee but add another. Check:

- *withdrawal fees*
- *currency conversion fees*
- *inactivity fees*
- *percentage-based account fees*
- *high brokerage on certain trades*

Zero fee does not always mean low cost.

WHAT'S NEXT?

Now that you understand how fees shape your long-term results, you're ready to explore crypto, one of the most talked-about—and misunderstood—parts of the modern money world.

You probably see promises of "easy money" everywhere: TikTok, Discord, YouTube, gaming chats, memes, and hype videos. Crypto can be fascinating, but it plays by completely different rules to the steady investing and low-fee strategies you've learned so far.

In the next chapter, we'll step calmly and clearly into this digital wild west. You'll learn what crypto actually is, why it's so volatile, how scams target young people, and how to stay safe if you ever decide to explore it in the future.

Up next: **SMART Crypto: Curiosity Welcome, Caution Essential**.

CHAPTER 10

SMART CRYPTO

"The time to repair the roof is when the sun is shining."

— John F. Kennedy

SMART Crypto: Curiosity Welcome, Caution Essential

> *"Explore new ideas, but never risk money you cannot afford to lose."*

Crypto is still a very new space. There is innovation and opportunity, but also confusion, hype, and risk. Learning how it works before putting money in is always the smartest first step.

Crypto is everywhere: in your feeds, group chats, memes, gaming communities, and ads promising outrageous returns. It feels futuristic, exciting, and powerful... and sometimes a bit secretive.

You'll probably hear about crypto before you ever hear about superannuation or ETFs. Crypto *is* interesting. It *is* new. And new things tend to come with both opportunity and chaos. This can be dangerous when you don't understand it.

This chapter isn't here to tell you to buy crypto. It's here so you don't get swept up in hype, pressure, or scams, and so you understand what crypto is before ever touching it. Crypto isn't "bad," it's just *different* from long-term investing. It behaves more like speculation or advanced-level risk, and if you ever choose to explore it, you should do so with eyes wide open.

Let's break it down clearly.

WHAT CRYPTO ACTUALLY IS—WITHOUT TECH-TALK

Crypto is a kind of digital money or digital asset stored on something called a blockchain.

A blockchain is basically:

- a giant digital spreadsheet
- stored on thousands of computers
- updated by everyone
- owned by no one

Because no single person controls it, people call it "decentralised," which means there's no central boss, bank, or company in charge. No one can freeze accounts, reverse mistakes, or step in to fix errors. That's part of the appeal, and part of the risk. And that should send your "Spidey senses" tingling. 🕷

That freedom comes with responsibility, and usually no help desk. As Uncle Ben tells Peter Parker in *Spider-Man*: "With great power comes great responsibility."

Here are some examples you've probably heard of:

- Bitcoin—digital gold
- Ethereum—the foundation of a lot of crypto apps
- Stablecoins—coins designed to stay at $1 (not always successfully)

Crypto isn't backed by a government or bank. Its price moves because of:

- hype
- supply and demand
- fear
- excitement

- global news
- influencers
- speculation

This makes crypto very volatile, which means prices can jump or crash *fast*.

SMART TIP

If you can't explain it simply, don't buy it (yet). If a crypto concept makes your brain fizz, that's your sign to learn more before putting your money in.

WHY CRYPTO FEELS SO EXCITING AND WHY YOU'RE TARGETED

Crypto pushes all the psychological buttons that make our brains light up:

- fast price swings
- flashy success stories
- "next big thing" energy
- community excitement
- the feeling of being early
- the idea you can get rich young

This combination makes crypto feel thrilling, sometimes more like a game than real money. Games are fun, but losing real money isn't. That's exactly why scammers love it. They know teens:

- are curious
- explore online spaces
- trust influencers

- learn by trying
- don't always know the red flags

Crypto scams are some of the fastest-growing scams in Australia and globally. But once you send your money, it's almost impossible to get it back.

> ⚠ WARNING
>
> **Crypto Is a Magnet for Scams**
>
> *Fake coins, fake exchanges, fake wallets, fake returns, fake influencers.*
>
> *If someone promises easy or guaranteed profits, they're not an expert, they're a threat. And if it feels rushed, secretive, or too good to be true, walk away. Run, even!*

HOW PEOPLE ACTUALLY BUY CRYPTO (SAFELY)

If you *ever* explore crypto in the future (with education and caution), here's how people usually buy it:

- **Choose a regulated exchange.** In Australia, that means an exchange registered with AUSTRAC. (Many foreign exchanges are unsafe or illegal.)
- **Verify your identity.** Just like opening a bank account.
- **Transfer money from your bank.** You use Australian dollars to buy crypto.
- **Store your crypto. Two main options:**
  - **Hot wallet:** connected to the internet (easy, but hackable)
  - **Cold wallet:** offline hardware device (safer, but requires care)

If you lose your password ("seed phrase"), your crypto is gone forever; "'Forgot my password"' is not a valid recovery plan in crypto. There's no customer service line with a reset button.

STORAGE EXPLAINED SIMPLY

Hot Wallets

These are apps or browser extensions that are convenient and good for beginners. **Risk:** if your phone is hacked, so is your wallet.

Cold Wallets

These are USB-like devices that store your crypto offline and are the safest option long-term. **Risk:** if you lose it *and* lose the recovery phrase, it's gone forever.

The tech is strong. Human memory is the weak link.

THE TRUE COSTS OF CRYPTO (STUFF NO ONE TELLS YOU)

Crypto has fees too:

- Exchange fees when you buy or sell
- Spread (the hidden difference between buy and sell prices)
- Gas fees (network fees, especially on Ethereum)
- Transfer fees between wallets
- Tax, because crypto gains are taxed like investments

Crypto isn't "free money," it's money with extra steps. You know, like money with homework.

REAL TALK

Crypto is not a shortcut to wealth. Most people who trade crypto lose money. Most teens who lose money never tell anyone. And no one brags about their losses online. Silence is not success.

TIPS AND TRAPS YOU SHOULD KNOW

- **Tip:** ***Start by learning, not buying.*** If you want to explore crypto, learn how it works first.
- **Tip:** ***Only ever use money you could lose without drama.*** Crypto behaves more like gambling than investing.
- **Trap:** ***Influencers don't know your situation.*** Much of the hype is paid promotion. Some don't even own the coins they promote.
- **Trap:** ***Fear of Missing Out (FOMO).*** FOMO is not a strategy, it's how people get wrecked. Again, if it feels urgent, pause.
- **Tip:** ***If someone DMs you about crypto, block them immediately***. No expert slides into your DMs to offer money-making tips. Ever. Not once. Not even accidentally.
- **Trap:** ***Fake romantic partners.*** Scammers build friendships, even relationships, then ask teens to buy crypto "for us."

Curiosity is healthy. Pressure is not. The following flowchart can help you tell the difference.

FLOWCHART—SHOULD I DO CRYPTO?

This flowchart isn't here to talk you *into* crypto. It's here to give you permission to say "not yet."

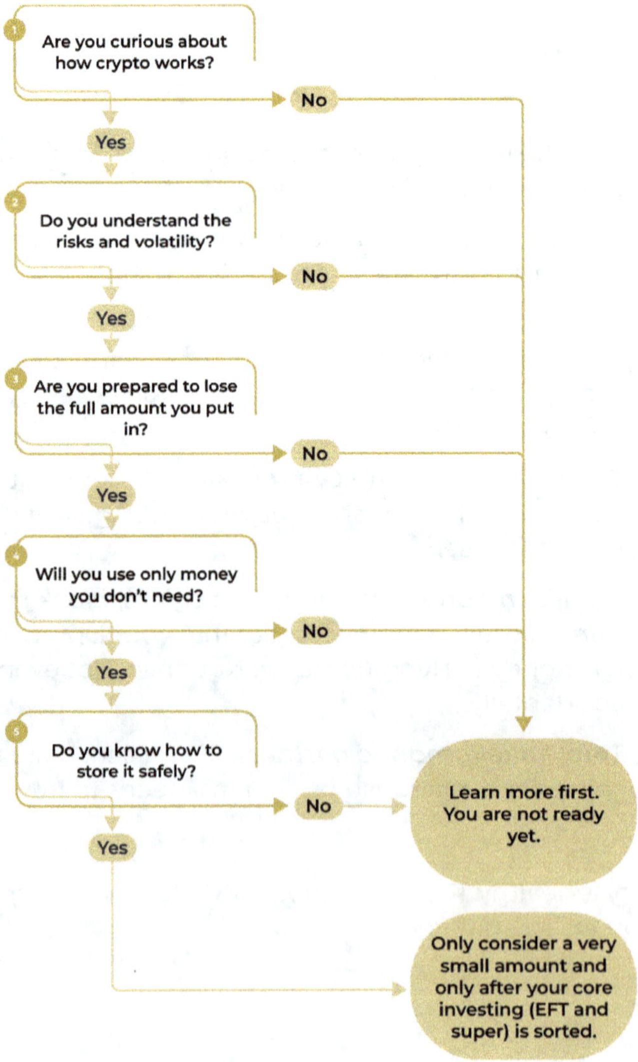

ACTIVITY: CRYPTO REALITY CHECK

- Why am I interested in crypto? ______________________________

Understanding

- Do I understand what blockchain is?
  Yes / No / Sort of
- Can I explain the coin I want to buy in simple terms?
  Yes / No

Risk

- Can I afford to lose 100% of this money?
  Yes / No
  If this question makes you uncomfortable, that's useful information. Pay attention to it.

Costs

- Do I understand the fees?
  Exchange fee: ______
  Spread: ______
  Gas fee: ______
  Withdrawal fee: ______
- Security
  How will I store it?
  Hot wallet (risk: hackable)
  Cold wallet (risk: lose access)

Safety

- Have I checked for scams?
  Website verified
  Not from a DM
  Not from a "guaranteed returns" post
  Not from an influencer I can't verify

WHEN CRYPTO FITS AND WHEN IT DOESN'T

Crypto is okay to explore *only* when:

- your savings habits are strong
- you understand investing basics
- your super is set up
- you have no debt
- you're using tiny amounts
- you accept the risk

Crypto is *not* appropriate when:

- you need the money back soon
- you're trying to "get rich fast"
- you're stressed, bored, lonely, or pressured
- someone else is pushing you
- you don't understand the tech
- you're using money you can't lose

Pressure is never a good reason to invest.

WHAT'S NEXT?

Crypto isn't good or bad, it's simply high risk and often misunderstood. If you decide to explore it one day, treat it as a side hobby rather than your main financial plan. And remember: Where there's excitement and fast money, there are also scams. Lots of them.

Next up we look at: **SMART Adulting: Everyday Skills That Make Life Less Chaotic.** This one is fun, practical, and filled with the kind of "why did nobody tell me this earlier?" moments that smooth the transition into independence.

CHAPTER 11

SMART ADULTING

"Prepare for the worst, but keep living for the best."

—Anne Lamott

SMART Adulting: Everyday Skills That Make Life Less Chaotic

> *"Adulting is just a collection of small skills that make life run more smoothly."*

There's a funny moment in life when you realise "adulting" isn't one big skill. It's a thousand tiny ones nobody ever bothered to explain properly. Like reading a payslip without staring at it in confusion, knowing why your phone bill doubled, or understanding why your tax return looks like it's written in ancient runes.

At one stage, my daughter decided that adulting was all a bit overwhelming and that I was a terrible parent for having her without her consent because she didn't want to adult. Again. Ever.

This chapter is your calm, friendly guide to the real-world basics that will make life smoother, cheaper and far less stressful.

Adulting doesn't mean knowing everything. It means knowing enough to stay in control, and understanding that you'll never stop learning.

READ YOUR PAYSLIP WITHOUT GUESSING

Payslips are small but mighty. They tell you:

- How many hours you were paid for
- Your hourly rate

- Your gross pay (before tax)
- Your net pay (after tax)
- How much tax was withheld
- Any penalty rates or allowances
- Any deductions
- Your superannuation
- Your year-to-date totals

Here are two things to check when you receive a payslip:

1. Did the employer record your hours correctly? Yes, mistakes do happen.

2. Is your super being paid? A tiny percentage now becomes a very large number later.

Taking a quick look at each payslip and occasionally checking that your super is being paid can prevent problems later.

UNDERSTANDING TAX: THE CALM, NO-PANIC VERSION

Tax isn't a punishment designed to get you, it's just how the system works. Here's the simplified version:

- If you earn money, you may pay tax
- The more you earn, the more tax you might pay
- When you lodge your tax return, the ATO checks whether you paid too much or too little
- If you overpaid → refund
- If you underpaid → bill

That's it! There's no need to memorise complicated tables or formulas.

Taxes feel like money that just disappears from your pay, but they're actually the fuel that keeps your whole community running. Every time you earn income, buy something, or fill up your car, a slice goes towards things you use every day without even noticing: roads, public transport, hospitals, schools, emergency services, parks, libraries, clean water, rubbish collection, and the people who keep all of that functioning.

They also help fund big safety nets like Centrelink, Medicare, disability support, and aged care, which step in when someone hits tough times. In other words, taxes are how we all chip in so society doesn't fall apart. It's not the most glamorous thing about earning money, but it's one of the ways you're connected to your community.

The moment you start paying taxes, you're playing a part in making your town, your state, and your country work.

The Tax File Number (TFN)

Your TFN identifies you with the ATO. Keep it private and secure and never give it out casually.

Income Statements

Employers lodge your income details with the ATO. You can see them through your myGov portal.

Tax Returns

You lodge one every year (either yourself or through an accountant). Look out for:

- income from jobs
- bank interest
- deductions you're allowed to claim

If in doubt, ask someone who knows. Tax stress is optional.

GETTING A TAX FILE NUMBER (TFN): WHAT IT IS AND WHY YOU NEED ONE

A Tax File Number (TFN) is your personal ID number with the Australian Tax Office. It's not exciting, but it is important. You need it for:

- starting a job
- being paid correctly
- avoiding extra tax
- opening a bank account
- getting a super fund
- doing a tax return
- enrolling in uni/TAFE (for HECS-HELP loans)

Without a TFN, you'll pay the highest tax rate automatically. It's the ATO's way of saying, "We're not sure who you are, so we're taking no chances." Having a TFN keeps everything straightforward.

How to Apply for a TFN

The good news? It's simple and free. If you're an Australian citizen or permanent resident, you can apply through the ATO website, which will take you through the steps. To apply for your TFN, you'll need ID, such as a:

- driver's licence or learner's permit
- passport
- Medicare card

It usually arrives in around 28 days, sometimes sooner. If you're under 18 and starting your first job, you can still apply yourself. Or ask a parent to help you with the ID check if needed.

If you're an international student or temporary resident, you can also apply through the ATO, using your passport and visa.

> **SMART TIP**
>
> *Never share your TFN casually. Treat it like your PIN. Only employers, banks, the ATO, and your super fund or some insurers should ever need it.*

WHY YOU REALLY NEED TO APPLY

Someone once started their first job without a TFN, thinking, "I'll sort it out later." They didn't.

When you don't hold a TFN, your employer will withhold the highest tax rate—and the money you earn is drastically reduced! While you can fix it later and get the extra tax refunded, doing this is annoying and frustrating. A TFN avoids all that drama.

As you move into adult life, money starts showing up in new places. Not just on payslips, but also in everyday expenses like phone plans, subscriptions, and utility bills. This leads us to an important skill: learning how to check a bill when something does not look quite right.

> **SMART TIP**
>
> *Good financial habits start with curiosity, not perfection.*

BILLS: WHY THEY DO WEIRD THINGS

There will come a day when a bill looks "wrong." It's practically a rite of passage. Is your electricity bill unusually high? Has your phone bill suddenly doubled? Are subscription fees mysteriously appearing?

Before panicking, check:

- Did your plan change?
- Did your data or power usage spike?
- Did an introductory discount end?
- Did someone accidentally stream 48 hours of HD video?
- Did you upgrade something without realising?

If a bill looks wrong, you can contact the provider and ask about it. Mistakes do happen, and they are usually easy to fix when they are caught early.

RENTING BASICS (EVEN IF YOU'RE NOT THERE YET)

Renting comes with:

- a lease (your rental contract)
- a bond (your refundable deposit)
- routine inspections
- rent due weekly, fortnightly, or monthly
- responsibility for keeping the place clean
- rules around noise, pets, damage, and subletting

Again, it is so important to be aware of your obligations and rights.

The biggest shock for most people is the upfront cost. Bond (often four weeks' rent), plus two to four weeks' rent in advance, plus utility connections, and sometimes moving costs, can add up quickly. Ouch.

Planning ahead helps.

It's also good to communicate with your flatmates up front about expectations. Will you take turns with the cooking and cleaning, or will each person have their own chores? Are you a neat freak with a laid-back buddy who loves a floor-drobe? Being clear up front can save issues later.

PHONE PLANS: THE SILENT BUDGET DESTROYER

Phone costs sneak up on people more than any other bill. Keep an eye on:

- data usage
- roaming charges overseas
- premium SMS services (usually accidental)
- device repayments hiding in the bill
- plans that quietly increase after 12 months

If a plan feels overpriced, it probably is. Before committing, compare a few things such as the monthly price, how much data you get, whether the plan locks you into a contract, and what happens if you go over your limit.

Loyalty rarely pays with telcos. Providers regularly offer better deals to attract new customers than to keep existing ones. Comparison sites such as WhistleOut or Finder can help you quickly see what different providers are charging in Australia.

> **SMART TIP**
>
> *A cheap bill is nice, but a predictable one may be better.*

CONTRACTS AND COMMITMENTS

Before you sign anything, ask yourself: *Do I fully understand what I'm agreeing to?* Then look for:

- minimum terms
- break fees
- hidden costs
- what happens if you miss a payment
- whether it auto-renews

Contracts don't have to be scary, they simply require a moment of your attention.

If you need to take time to work through it, or ask for help to better understand, don't be afraid to ask. If you're ever pressured to "sign or the deal evaporates," walk away. Chances are, you can do better elsewhere.

BANKING

A few habits that will save you money:

- Review your statements monthly
- Cancel unused subscriptions
- Track your spending occasionally
- Keep bills organised
- Check interest charges
- Update passwords
- Don't store passwords in your Notes app (tempting, but risky)

These tiny habits stop bigger problems later.

MADDY'S PHONE PLAN

Maddy ignored her emailed phone bill for three months because the emails "looked boring." She just saved them in a folder in her inbox.

By the time she finally reviewed one, after wondering why the amount taken from her account was so high, she discovered:

- a forgotten device repayment
- a direct debit gone wrong
- late fees
- a premium text service they activated when she downloaded a wallpaper at midnight

A five-minute check each month could have saved her hundreds of dollars.

Adulting is not about being perfect. It's about paying attention, asking questions, and fixing things early.

ACTIVITY: LIFE ADMIN POWER HOUR

Choose one day this week, or even each month to complete a "Life Admin Power Hour."

Tick as many of these as you can:

- [ ] Look at one recent payslip
- [ ] Check your bank statement
- [ ] Review your phone bill
- [ ] Log into your super fund
- [ ] Cancel one subscription you don't use
- [ ] Change one old password
- [ ] Organise a digital folder for important documents
- [ ] Update your contact details (ATO, bank, employer)

One hour now saves many hours later.

WHAT'S NEXT?

Life skills make everything smoother, but there's still one area that can quietly make, or completely break, your financial wellbeing: *Relationships*. Money is emotional. Money involves friends, family, partners, even strangers online who don't stay strangers for long. And money can blur boundaries faster than almost anything else.

Most financial stress doesn't come from bad maths. It comes from pressure, trust misplaced, silence, guilt, fear, or not knowing when—or how—to say no.

Good boundaries help to keep you safe. They protect your money, your confidence, and your future choices.

Next up is: **Chapter 12: SMART Safety: Avoid Scams, Schemes, and Online Traps.** Because learning how to spot danger early, trust your instincts, and protect yourself isn't fear-based, it's one of the smartest life skills you'll ever learn.

CHAPTER 12

SMART SAFETY

"If something feels wrong, it usually is."

—Unknown

SMART Safety: Avoid Scams, Schemes, and Online Traps

> *"Good opportunities survive a pause. Scams rarely do."*

Money helps you build a good life, which means it may also attract people who want to take advantage of you:

- Some use charm
- Some use pressure
- Some use fake websites or messages that look legitimate
- Some promise "quick cash," "easy wins," or "guaranteed returns." ANY sentence that includes the word *guaranteed* deserves immediate suspicion.

SMART Safety isn't about paranoia, it's about awareness—the calm kind that notices things before they become problems. It's about recognising danger early, trusting your instincts, and protecting your accounts, identity, boundaries, and wellbeing.

WHY SCAMS WORK ON SMART PEOPLE

Scammers don't target "naïve" people. They target everyone, because their tools are emotional, not logical. And scammers succeed because they're:

- fast
- confident
- great storytellers
- emotionally skilled

- tech-savvy
- manipulative

Doctors, engineers, lawyers, students—highly educated adults fall for scams every day. Getting scammed doesn't mean you're foolish, it means someone was convincing.

Very convincing people exist. That's the risk. Your job is to learn to spot them early.

> **SMART TIP**
> *If a message makes your heart race—slow down. Scammers rely on panic, not logic. Urgency is a scammer's favourite shortcut.*

THE MOST COMMON SCAMS YOU'LL SEE

1. Fake Shopping Websites

Unbelievable discounts. Flash sales. "Only 2 left!" The internet somehow always has just *two* left, They take your money, but nothing arrives.

How to stay safe:

- check reviews
- search for real contact info
- avoid deals that feel unreal

2. Hacked Social Media Accounts

A message "from a friend" asking for:

- codes
- money

- bank transfers
- "urgent help"

If anything feels off, call your friend. Real friends won't be annoyed that you checked. Also, never share verification codes and turn on two-factor authentication everywhere.

3. Investment Scams

They promise:

- guaranteed returns
- no risk
- fast profits
- insider knowledge

If someone wants you to invest urgently or secretly, *walk away immediately*. Real investments will still exist tomorrow.

Red flags:

- pressure
- secrecy
- avoiding simple questions
- charts you don't understand
- friends bragging about profits they can't explain

4. Romance and Friendship Scams

Scammers build trust slowly: compliments → shared interests → emotional bonding. Then comes the request for:

- money
- crypto
- help with "urgent problems"
- intimate images

They use your kindness against you. Kindness is a strength, but it does need boundaries,

5. Subscription Traps

These often take the form of apps that appear free but quietly charge you after a trial period expires. These small fees add up fast, especially when you forget they exist.

6. Phone and Email Scams ("Phishing")

Fake messages pretending to be:

- your bank
- the ATO
- a parcel service
- Netflix, Amazon, etc.

They want you to click a link. Don't. Links are how scammers get invited inside.

How to stay safe:

- Log in through the official app, not the message.

7. The Grandparent Scam (And Why You Should Tell Your Family About It)

A scammer pretends to be a panicked grandchild needing urgent money. They rely on:

- fear
- confusion
- love

The goal is to make you act quickly without checking the story. Real emergencies can always be verified. The best protection is talking openly with your family and letting them know: "If anyone ever calls asking for money urgently, call me first, even if they sound like me. And I'll do the same with you." You can also consider creating a family password that only real family members know.

SMART TIP

Scammers rely on secrecy. Telling your family how these scams work is one of the best ways to protect them.

PRESSURE, MANIPULATION, AND "MONEY GUILT"

Not all financial danger comes from strangers, sometimes it comes from people you know.

Signs someone is pushing your boundaries:

- they pressure you to lend money
- they make you feel guilty for saying no
- they want access to your accounts
- they ask for passwords
- they take money and promise repayment "later"
- they speak over you in financial conversations
- they dismiss your concerns
- they get angry when you ask questions

You don't need to justify your boundaries to anyone. A simple "I can't do that" is enough. Explanations are optional. Boundaries are not. As Oprah says, **"No** is a complete sentence."

SMART BOUNDARIES FOR MONEY

These rules will protect you:

- Never lend money you can't afford to lose.
- Never share passwords or security codes.
- Don't let guilt push you into choices that harm you.
- Trust your discomfort—your instincts are often right.

Your gut will notice patterns before your brain explains them.

THE DODGY FRIEND

Ever had that friend who "forgot their wallet" every time they went out? The amounts grew: $10... $20... $40... Eventually they asked for hundreds "just for a few days."

And when you finally said no, the friend disappeared.

Healthy relationships do not rely on financial pressure. If money is the glue, it won't hold.

ONLINE SAFETY: PROTECT YOUR DIGITAL WALLET

A few simple habits make your money much safer online:

- use two-factor authentication everywhere
- use strong, unique passwords
- update your apps
- avoid public Wi-Fi for banking
- don't save cards on every website
- check bank statements regularly
- lock your SIM card with a PIN

These tiny habits prevent big disasters.

CRYPTO, TRADING, AND "QUICK MONEY" TRAPS

Crypto is exciting, which is why scammers love it.

Red flags:

- someone else asks you to invest
- they want remote access to your computer
- they promise guaranteed return
- they ask you to download special apps
- they ask for screenshots of your wallet
- they ask you to keep the opportunity secret

Legitimate investing doesn't require secrecy, pressure, or confusion. Calm money decisions age better than exciting ones.

HOW TO SPOT A SCAM IN 10 SECONDS

Ask yourself:

- Does it feel urgent? → Scam
- Is it too good to be true? → Scam
- Do they avoid clear answers? → Scam
- Are they asking for secrecy? → Scam
- Do they want access to your device? → Scam
- Does something feel off? → Scam

Trust your instincts; they are often smarter than you think. You just need to listen the first time!

WHAT TO DO IF YOU FALL FOR A SCAM

It happens. To smart people. All the time.

You are not stupid.
You are not alone.
You are not to blame for someone else's dishonesty.

Take action immediately:

- contact your bank
- change your passwords
- secure your email
- report to ReportCyber or Scamwatch
- talk to someone you trust

Shame is a scammer's favourite tool, and speaking up breaks their power.

ACTIVITY: THE "WOULD I TELL A FRIEND?" TEST

Think of a money decision you're unsure about.

Ask yourself: "If my best friend told me they were about to do this, what advice would I give them?"

That answer is usually the right one. We're often wiser for others than ourselves.

WHAT'S NEXT?

You now know how to protect your money, your accounts, and your boundaries. But some of the most dangerous traps young people face aren't about money, they're about trust, images, pressure, and emotional manipulation.

In the next chapter, we'll dive into sextortion, online grooming, and the psychological tools scammers use to trick, shame, or control teens. This is one of the fastest-growing threats worldwide and understanding it now puts you miles ahead.

Up next: **SMART Socials—Understand the Tools Predators and Scammers Use, and How to Stay Safe Online**. Awareness now is protection later.

CHAPTER 13

SMART SOCIALS

"Your worth isn't measured by what you share, it's measured by who you are."

—Unknown

SMART Socials: Understand the Tools Predators and Scammers Use, and How to Stay Safe Online

> *"Your future deserves protection, even from the moments you think won't matter."*

SEXTORTION: WHEN FEAR BECOMES A WEAPON

Sextortion isn't really about sex. It's about control, panic, and profit. And right now, young people across Australia are being targeted because they're online, spontaneous, and still learning who to trust.

This chapter isn't here to frighten you. It's here to take something that feels terrifying and makes it survivable. Knowledge turns panic into options.

HOW THE TRAP STARTS

Most sextortion begins somewhere familiar, like Snapchat, Instagram, TikTok, Discord, or gaming chats. A new add. A friendly message. Someone who seems to be your age. Someone who talks like a teen. They're scripted to sound just like you. They've practiced sounding just right.

Then the script starts.

WDYLL?
Got a pic?

DYS?
You're cute. Thought you were older.
Show me something quick before this disappears.

None of this is spontaneous. These lines are lifted from playbooks used in organised criminal operations. They're designed to speed you up, flatter you, and stop you thinking too hard. Scripts beat improvisation every time. And once an image is sent, everything changes.

THE SHAME TRAP

The tone flips instantly:
Send money or I'll post this everywhere.
Do it now or your whole school will see.

Suddenly your stomach drops. Your brain hits panic mode. You imagine worst-case scenarios. And paying money to stop this can seem like the only way out. It never is. Silence is the leverage. Speaking up removes it.

Once they know you're scared, they will push for more: more money, more photos, more control. This panic is why some teenagers have made heartbreaking decisions. But shame only works when you stay silent. You are never alone in this.

THE DIGITAL TRUTH NO ONE WANTS TO HEAR

Once an image leaves your phone, you lose control of it. There's also something important many young people don't realise: If you are under 16, creating, possessing, or sharing sexual images of yourself or other minors is illegal, even if it was consensual.

That means anyone threatening to share images of a minor is committing a serious crime. You are not the one in trouble. They are. Even on disappearing-photo apps. "Disappearing" is a promise, not a guarantee, because people screenshot and screen record. People save things secretly and yes, images can follow you into your future, to jobs, traineeships, and uni programs. Employers check digital footprints, not to punish you, but because the internet remembers everything. Protecting your privacy now protects your future self. Future You will never regret caution.

ROHAN'S STORY

In Victoria, seventeen-year-old Rohan Cosgriff was targeted on Snapchat by someone using the name "Christine." After being pressured to send an intimate image, he was blackmailed. The account was traced overseas.

Sadly, Rohan died by suicide in 2022.

His family now shares his story, so no young person will feel trapped in fear the way he did.

The State Coroner later said that young people must know that if this happens, it will be OK and help is available. A mistake doesn't define you. There is always a way forward.

Help works. Silence doesn't. His story is painful, but it reminds us that silence is the dangerous part.

IMPORTANT TO KNOW (ESPECIALLY IF YOU'RE UNDER 16)

In Australia, the law recognises that under-16s need extra protection online.

If you are under 16 and someone pressures, threatens, or blackmails you for images, *you are not at fault,* even if you sent something voluntarily. The responsibility lies entirely with the adult or criminal exploiting you.

This is why telling a trusted adult immediately is so important: the law is on *your* side.

WHAT TO DO IF IT HAPPENS

- Stay calm
- Don't pay
- Take screenshots
- Block the person
- Report them inside the app
- Lodge a report with the eSafety Commissioner
- Tell a trusted adult immediately

Most threats aren't carried out once the criminal realises you're not cooperating. Control disappears when fear does. If you're under 16, authorities and platforms treat this as child exploitation and act quickly to protect you. The laws exist here to protect you, not to shame you. eSafety, the Australian Federal Police and state police all prioritise image removal and protection. They can get help content removed quickly, and adults can step in long before anything spirals.

Remember, you were never in a real relationship. They don't require secrecy, speed, or pressure.

Nothing is so bad it can't be fixed. This moment does NOT get to define you.

> **SMART TIP**
>
> *If you're under 16 and someone has sexual images of you, the law is on your side. Don't negotiate. Don't pay. Get help immediately.*

BEHIND THE SCAMS

Many sextortion threats don't come from anyone local. A large number originate from trafficking compounds in Cambodia, Myanmar, and Laos where people are kidnapped or tricked into fake jobs. They are locked inside gated buildings and forced to work long hours sending scam messages under threat of violence. They aren't villains, they're victims too. Exploited people are often used to exploit others.

The real criminals are the syndicates that make millions by exploiting both sides: the teens being blackmailed and the adults trapped inside. Understanding this helps dissolve blame. You weren't tricked by a flirt, you were targeted by a machine. And machines don't care who you are, which means this was never personal.

YOU'RE "JUST HAVING A BIT OF FUN"

A lot of sextortion begins in the same emotional space as early romance scams. Someone compliments you, flirts, and makes you feel interesting or special.

At first it feels harmless. You're not dating. You're not planning anything serious. You're just chatting. Everyone chats. This is exactly why the setup works .Trust first. Pressure later. Not because you're naïve, but because you're human. And being human is your great asset. It's NOT a flaw.

Yahoo Boys

Yahoo Boys are organised scam groups, mostly based in parts of West Africa who specialise in online manipulation. Their name comes from the early days of internet scams in Nigeria, when many fraudsters used Yahoo email accounts to run fake lotteries, romances, and investment schemes. The name stuck, even as the scams became far more sophisticated. They run everything from romance scams to fake investments, sextortion, phishing and "quick cash" schemes. Their whole strategy is built on studying how people think and react online.

Psychology is their weapon. They use stolen photos, pretend to be influencers or love interests, mimic banks or parcel companies, and push emotional buttons like urgency, guilt, or flattery to get money, gift cards, or personal info.

Teens are often targeted because Yahoo Boys assume you're online a lot, trusting, and quick to respond. Knowing their patterns—sudden compliments from strangers, love-bombing, pressure to keep secrets, requests for money, or offers that feel way too good to be true—helps you spot their tricks instantly.

The more familiar you are with how these scams work, the harder you are to manipulate. Knowledge is your shield. Patterns lose power once you can name them.

Pig Butchering

Pig butchering scams take their name from the Chinese phrase "杀猪盘" (shā zhū pán) which literally translates to "pig-killing plate." It comes from underground slang used by criminal networks in China and Southeast Asia, and describes the method of "fattening up" a victim with trust, affection, and fake profits before "slaughtering" them by emptying their savings. The scam usually starts with a friendly or flirty message from a stranger, sometimes on Instagram, Snapchat, gaming platforms, even just a random "wrong number" text.

The scammer slowly builds a relationship, makes you feel chosen, special, and safe... then introduces the "opportunity:" crypto trading, investment apps, or money-making platforms that look legitimate but are completely fake.

You see fake earnings, fake graphs, fake success stories, all designed to convince you to put in more. Once you've invested everything they think they can get, they block you, vanish, or shut down the fake platform. That's "slaughter." The cruelty is deliberate and the manipulation is calculated.

Knowing about pig butchering and the behaviour behind it helps you recognise the pattern early. If someone online is pushing fast intimacy, secret conversations, or "guaranteed" returns, you are not dealing with a friend. You are being fattened for a scam.

PROTECTION WITHOUT QUITTING SOCIALS

You don't need to disappear offline to stay safe.

- Keep your accounts private
- Avoid random adds with no mutuals
- Trust your instincts
- Block early

Being cautious doesn't make you boring, it makes you harder to manipulate. It makes you smart.

This is the truth you deserve to hear: You're not stupid. You're not in trouble. You're not ruined. Sadly, you're not the only one this has happened to.

There is always a way out. There is always someone who can help. Your future matters too much to let criminals shape the story.

SMART TIP

If someone online rushes you, pressures you, or flips from friendly to demanding, end the chat early. Real connections never need urgency. Pressure is never a sign of care.

WARNING

If someone threatens to share your images, don't pay and don't hide. Screenshot, block, report and tell a trusted adult immediately. Most threats are never carried out. Paying feeds the cycle. Reporting stops it.

WHAT'S NEXT?

You've learned how to recognise danger, protect your boundaries, and respond when something doesn't feel right.

That awareness is powerful.

But safety isn't only about scams, strangers, or online threats; sometimes it's about life throwing curveballs you didn't plan for, like illness, injury, accidents, or sudden disruptions that have nothing to do with bad choices and everything to do with being human.

That's where insurance comes in. Insurance isn't about fear or worst-case thinking, it's about creating a safety net so one tough moment doesn't undo years of effort.

In the next chapter, **SMART Insurance: Protect Your Health and Your Stuff**, we'll break down what insurance does (without jargon), which types matter when you're young, which ones don't, and how the right cover quietly protects your income, independence, and future choices.

You've learned how to spot risk. Now you'll learn how to soften the impact when life inevitably throws a plot twist.

CHAPTER 14

SMART INSURANCE

"Hope is not a strategy."

- Dr. Emily Chang

SMART Insurance: Protect Your Health and Your Stuff

> *"Money is partly about building your future...and partly about protecting it."*

Insurance steps in when life throws an unexpected plot twist like an accident, an illness, a broken phone, a stolen bike, a hospital visit, or something far more challenging such as losing the ability to work. It doesn't remove the problem itself, but it stops a bad situation from becoming a financial earthquake.

Think of insurance as a shock absorber for your life. You'll still hit bumps, but just maybe, the wheels won't fall off.

> **SMART TIP**
>
> *Insurance protects your money, possessions, income, health, and your peace of mind.*

WHY IT MATTERS

Life is full of "that will never happen to me" moments—right up until they do.

A cracked laptop.
A stolen bike.
A broken arm.
A prang in a car park.
A visit to emergency on a Sunday night.

It doesn't take much for a small slip to become a big expense.

Insurance is the tool that keeps you standing when the unexpected tries to knock you flat. At its core, insurance does one thing: *It replaces money at the exact moment you need it most.*

THE TWO BIG AREAS OF INSURANCE

1. General Insurance: Protects your belongings and your day-to-day life.

2. Personal Insurance: Protects *you*, your health, your income, and the people who rely on you.

Both matter. But maybe not just yet.

Personal insurance is where the real long-term life-changing protection sits.

GENERAL INSURANCE

Your Stuff, Your Wheels, Your World

Car Insurance

Once you're driving, this becomes essential.

- **Compulsory Third Party (CTP)** – covers injuries to people if you cause an accident
- **Third Party Property** – covers damage you cause to someone else's car or property
- **Comprehensive** – covers your car, their car, storms, theft, accidents, and sometimes fire

In most Australian states CTP is included when you pay your vehicle registration. In New South Wales it is purchased separately and is commonly called a "Green Slip." CTP only covers injuries to people. It does not cover damage to cars or property. A single accident can cost years of earnings. Car insurance stops that from derailing your future.

Contents Insurance

Protect your belongings. If your laptop, phone, jewellery, musical instruments, sports gear, or furniture are stolen, damaged, or lost, contents insurance helps replace them. If you're renting or moving out of home, this becomes very useful.

Home Insurance

Protects the building itself: walls, roof, fixtures, repairs, rebuild costs. If you ever own property, this becomes essential.

Travel Insurance

The overlooked hero of every trip. Whether you're faced with lost luggage, cancelled flights, food poisoning, delayed connections, or emergency medical treatment, travel insurance turns chaos into inconvenience instead of a $10,000 nightmare.

Pet Insurance

Vet bills can rival human hospital costs these days. Pet insurance helps cover illness, accidents, medication, and surgery, which is especially helpful for unexpected emergencies.

Phone and Gadget Insurance

Lost phone? Smashed laptop? These policies help replace essential tech quickly, especially if you rely on it for work or study.

Extended Warranty and Accidental Damage Cover

Often available when buying electronics or appliances, these are usually only worthwhile for very high-value items.

CROWD FUNDING

Crowd funding is sometimes promoted as a cheaper, more flexible alternative to traditional insurance.

This is where a group of people contribute small amounts into a shared pool and, when someone experiences a loss, the community votes or approves payments from the fund. It can feel modern and collaborative, but it comes with a hard truth: *Payouts are not guaranteed.* If the group decides not to support your claim, or there simply isn't enough money in the pool, you're left with the full cost yourself.

Crowd funding should never replace proper insurance for serious events because it's unpredictable, highly risky and, ultimately, relies on others' goodwill to bail you out. Relying on charity to get through adversity isn't financial independence, it's the opposite of adulting.

Community goodwill is lovely. A guaranteed payout is better.

HOW PERSONAL INSURANCE FITS TOGETHER

This is a simple way to picture it:

- **Life** – protects your family
- **Total and Permanent Disability (TPD)** – protects your future
- **Trauma** – protects your recovery
- **Income Protection** – protects your ability to earn an income.

Together, they form a financial shield around your life.

PERSONAL INSURANCE

This is the part of insurance that protects your wellbeing and your long-term financial stability. It's about *you*. And just as you suspected, you're surprisingly expensive to replace.

1. Life Insurance

- Pays a lump sum if you die or become terminally ill.
- Supports the people who depend on you: your partner, children, parents, anyone relying on your financial contribution.
- Gives your loved ones breathing room at the worst moment of their lives.

2. Total and Permanent Disability (TPD) Insurance

Pays a lump sum if an illness or injury means you can't ever return to work.

ELLIOT'S STORY

Elliot suffered a brain injury from a bike crash. He could no longer work in his profession. His TPD payout allowed him to modify his home, reduce financial pressure, and focus on rehab.

Without it, he would have faced medical bills, lost income, and ongoing costs while dealing with a devastating injury.

3. Trauma / Critical Illness Insurance

Provides a lump sum if diagnosed with a serious condition such as:

- cancer
- heart attack
- stroke
- MS
- major surgeries
- neurological conditions

It's your freedom fund while you focus on recovery.

AISHA'S STORY

Aisha was 27 when diagnosed with thyroid cancer. Her trauma insurance meant she could take four months off work, pay rent, cover medical costs, and travel interstate for specialist care, without draining her savings.

4. Income Protection Insurance

If you're working, this one is a game changer because it replaces part of your income if you can't work due to illness or injury (after a waiting period). This is the safety net that keeps the lights on, rent paid, and food in the fridge during your recovery.

LUCAS' STORY

Lucas fractured his hand in a bike accident and couldn't work for eight weeks. Income protection kept his wages flowing until he healed. He got four weeks of pay after his obligatory four week waiting period. He could also claim on his sick leave from work to cover part of the waiting period.

INSURANCE INSIDE SUPER VS OUTSIDE SUPER

This is a critical distinction most people don't understand: Superannuation can hold Life, TPD, and sometimes Income Protection. Trauma can't be owned in your super.

Insurance Inside Super

Pros:

- Premiums come from super balance, not your bank account
- Often cheaper due to group rates
- Easy to set up

Cons:

- Benefits may be taxed
- Definitions can be more restrictive
- Claims must meet *super laws*, not just insurance rules
- Reduces your retirement savings over time

Insurance Outside Super

Pros:

- Usually stronger definitions
- Faster claims process
- Trauma insurance available
- Benefits often tax-free
- Doesn't erode your super balance

Cons:

- Premiums paid from your own pocket
- Can be more expensive

A Smart Blended Approach

Many people use a mix:

- Basic Life/TPD inside super
- Stronger Life/TPD or Trauma outside super
- Income Protection based on quality and affordability

This creates efficient cover without sacrificing quality or affordability.

> **SMART TIP**
>
> *Protect what would be financially devastating—not the things you can easily replace.*

HOW INSURANCE FITS INTO YOUR MONEY PLAN

Insurance doesn't help you grow wealth, it protects the wealth you're building. It keeps your financial plan intact when life tries to tear it apart, and protects your biggest assets, your:

- ability to earn
- future goals
- family
- savings
- super
- independence

Insurance is the fence that protects the house while you're building it.

WHAT TO LOOK FOR (AND WHAT TO AVOID)

Look for:

- Clear definitions
- Strong claims history
- Fair premiums
- Flexibility
- Transparency

Avoid:

- Exclusions buried in fine print
- Policies you don't understand
- Cheap policies that won't pay when needed
- Insurance overlap (paying twice for the same cover)

YOUR INSURANCE CHECKLIST

- [ ] **Do you rely on your income?** Income Protection
- [ ] **Would someone struggle financially if you died?** Life Insurance
- [ ] **Would long-term disability change everything?** TPD Insurance
- [ ] **Would a major illness disrupt your life?** Trauma Insurance
- [ ] **Do you own your home?** Home + Contents Insurance
- [ ] **Do you rent your home?** Contents Insurance
- [ ] **Drive a vehicle?** Car Insurance
- [ ] **Have a pet?** Pet Insurance
- [ ] **Travel?** Travel Insurance

The point isn't to insure everything, just the things you can't easily replace.

THE REALITY OF CLAIMS

In difficult moments, insurance can feel like a lifeline. But claims run smoother when you understand:

Excess—What you pay first before insurance covers the rest.

Waiting periods—The time before your benefit starts (especially in income protection).

Exclusions—Things not covered (activities, pre-existing conditions, high-risk behaviours).

Definitions—Especially in TPD and Trauma, the exact wording matters.

Knowing this upfront avoids heartache later.

HOW TO MAKE A CLAIM

- Stay calm.
- Gather evidence—photos, receipts, reports.
- Contact the insurer as soon as practical.
- Give clear, accurate details.
- Politely but consistently follow up if needed.

Most claims aren't personal. They're processes. The clearer the information, the faster the payout.

COMMON MISCONCEPTIONS

"I'm young, nothing will happen." Hospitals and rehab clinics tell a different story every day.

"Insurance is too expensive." Losing your income is *far* more expensive.

"My savings will cover it." A single medical event can wipe out years of savings.

"If something happens, my family will just help." They will try, but they shouldn't have to carry the financial burden too. Love is not a financial plan.

THE BOTTOM LINE

Insurance isn't about pessimism. It's about protecting your options, your future, and your freedom. You don't buy insurance because you expect disaster, you buy it so disaster can't destroy your financial life.

That's smart.
That's strong.
That's how you protect the life you're building.

📔 ACTIVITY: YOUR PROTECTION CHECKLIST

Write down the items or areas in your life that would be painful to replace or deal with financially.

Tick the ones you want to protect right now:

- ☐ Income 💰
- ☐ Car 🏎️
- ☐ Phone 📱
- ☐ Laptop 💻
- ☐ Health 😷
- ☐ Travel 🛫
- ☐ Home / contents 🏡
- ☐ Pets 🐶
- ☐ Valuables 💍
- ☐ Life protection for loved ones 👨‍👩‍👧

This becomes your personal insurance blueprint.

You won't need it all at once, so don't stress. And hopefully, the parentals will continue to help pick up the slack for a few years to come.

WHAT'S NEXT?

You've now learned how to earn money, manage it, grow it, protect it, and keep it safe from people and situations that could derail you.

Insurance isn't about fear, it's about stability.

It's the quiet layer of protection that keeps one bad moment from undoing years of effort. The fence around what you're building. The backup plan you hope you never need, but are deeply glad exists.

Once protection is in place, everything else feels lighter: You can make choices with more confidence. You can take opportunities without constant "what if?" stress. With the safety net sorted, it's time to shift focus from protection to purpose.

Up next: **Chapter 15—SMART Goals: Build A Life You're Proud Of**.

Money is most powerful when it supports something meaningful. The goals you set and the life you want to build will guide how you earn, save, spend, and invest.

CHAPTER 15

SMART GOALS

"The secret of getting ahead is getting started."

—Mark Twain

SMART Goals: Build A Life You're Proud Of

> *"Small choices, repeated often, quietly build the life you end up living."*

Money isn't the goal. A good life is. And a good life looks different for everyone, depending on your perspective on: adventure, stability, success, creativity, security, contribution, freedom, family, travel, growth. Whatever matters to you deserves time, attention, and planning.

This chapter helps you turn vague "someday" ideas into something clearer, kinder, and far more achievable. Goals don't have to be loud or dramatic, they just need to be yours.

WHY GOALS MATTER (EVEN WHEN LIFE CHANGES)

Goals give you direction. They make your choices easier, help you say "yes" or "no" with more confidence, and help money become a tool, not a stress or a mystery.

You don't need to map out your whole life. You just need to know what you want next, and how to take the first step.

Think of goals as signposts to guide you.

THE SMART FRAMEWORK

Smart Goals become more powerful when they're:

Specific—clear and well-defined

Measurable—you can track progress

Achievable—realistic for your life

Relevant—meaningful to you

Time-bound—with a timeframe

Smart Goals don't box you in, they give your dreams a handle.

EXAMPLES OF SMART GOALS

"Save $1,000 for a new laptop over six months by putting away $35-$40 a week." Clear, simple, and doable.

"Put $20 a week into my travel fund so I'll have spending money in Japan next year." Future joy funded by tiny habits.

"Pay back my mini loan from Mum by the end of the school term." Responsibility feels surprisingly good when you complete it. And it's likely Mum will trust you and be there again if you ever need her help.

"Work 2–3 shifts over the Christmas holidays to build my savings to $1,200." Cashflow on purpose.

THE POWER OF CLARITY

Two friends set a goal to "save money." One wrote down a number whereas the other kept it vague.

Guess who succeeded? The one with the number.

Not because they were more disciplined, but because their brain knew what it was trying to achieve. Clarity beats willpower every time.

FINDING YOUR WHY

Behind every goal is a reason—something meaningful that motivates you.

Ask yourself: *Why do I want this*? Is it for:

- Freedom?
- Stability?
- Travel?
- Security?
- Opportunity?
- Pride?
- Helping someone you love?

The stronger your "why," the easier the habits become. Money without meaning is boring. Money with meaning is powerful.

LONG-TERM VS. SHORT-TERM GOALS

You need both.

Short-term goals (0–12 months)

- new phone
- weekend trip
- upgrading your laptop
- building an emergency buffer
- saving for something fun

These keep you motivated and give you wins along the way.

Long-term goals (1–10+ years)

- buying a car
- travel
- starting a business
- owning a home
- financial independence
- career milestones

These guide your big decisions, study, work, savings, and habits.

> **SMART TIP**
>
> *Short-term goals give you momentum. Long-term goals give you direction.*

HOW TO CHOOSE GOALS THAT STICK

1. Keep them personal

Not what your parents want.
Not what your friends want.
What you want.

2. Keep them realistic

Aiming for $10,000 savings on a part-time job might not work. Aiming for $1,000 absolutely can.

3. Keep them flexible

Your goals will evolve as you grow. That's not failure—that's development.

4. Keep them visible

Goals hidden in a drawer get forgotten. Put them where you see them: journal, phone wallpaper, sticky note, whiteboard.

MONEY GOALS VS. LIFE GOALS

Not all goals involve money. Some just make your life better. They:

- improve mental health
- develop a new skill
- strengthen friendships
- improve fitness
- develop confidence
- build routines

Money supports these goals, but doesn't replace them.

ACTIVITY: HOW TO BETTER UNDERSTAND YOURSELF

Write down three things:

1. Something you want to have (car, savings, travel, degree)

____

____

2. Something you want to do (hike a trail, learn a skill, start a podcast)

____

____

3. Someone you want to become (confident, creative, independent, healthier)

____

____

That third one? That's the big one. Goals built around who you want to become always last longer.

WHEN GOALS CHANGE (BECAUSE THEY WILL)

Changing your mind is allowed. Growing out of a goal is normal. Realising you want something different is healthy.

A goal isn't a contract, it's a guide. The important part is setting goals, not freezing your life around them forever.

> **SMART TIP**
>
> *Goals don't have to be perfect. They just have to be started.*

TURNING GOALS INTO ACTION

A goal without a plan is a daydream; it might be lovely, but it's not very useful. Break your goal into steps:

Goal: Save $800 for a laptop.

Steps:

- open a savings bucket
- set up an automatic transfer of $35/week
- track progress monthly
- avoid impulse spending
- celebrate when you hit milestones

Small steps beat huge intentions every single time.

WHEN MOTIVATION DIES (BECAUSE IT WILL)

It's normal to feel excited at the start and tired in the middle. A few tricks that help:

- review your "why"
- make steps smaller
- remove distractions
- ask for accountability
- give yourself rewards
- recommit without guilt

Perfection is optional. Persistence is powerful. And restarting when you need to counts as persistence.

📒 ACTIVITY: YOUR THREE SMART GOALS

Write down:

- [ ] One short-term goal (0–12 months)

___
___
___

- [ ] One medium-term goal (1–3 years)

___
___
___

- [ ] One long-term goal (3–10 years)

___
___
___

- [ ] Then add one sentence for each: *Why do I want this?*

___
___
___

Put it somewhere you'll see it.

WHAT'S NEXT?

You've learned how money works, how to earn it, spend it, save it, protect it, grow it, and use technology without letting it use you. Now comes the most important part: bringing it all together.

SMART Money: Making It All Work for You is where everything you've learned connects into one clear, personal system. This chapter isn't about rules or perfection, it's about shaping a money life that fits *you*—your values, goals, habits, boundaries, and the life you want to live.

This is where money stops feeling like a collection of topics and starts working as a calm, supportive tool in the background of your life.

CHAPTER 16

SMART MONEY

"You are what you repeatedly do."

—Aristotle (attributed)

SMART Money: Making It All Work For You

> *"A money plan is simply a way of turning your values into daily choices."*

You've now learned how to earn, save, spend, bank, invest, protect, grow, and guard your money. Chapter by chapter, you've built skills most adults learn the hard way. So now it's time to put everything together into something powerful: a personal money plan that makes your life easier, calmer and more intentional.

A money plan isn't a strict rulebook, it's a living guide that is simple, flexible and built around what you want your life to look like.

WHAT A MONEY PLAN ACTUALLY IS

It's not a spreadsheet, a strict budget, or a set of rules that punish you for being human. Your money plan is: *How I want my money to help me live the life I want.*

It includes your:

- goals
- habits
- priorities
- boundaries
- buckets
- values

- future plans
- real-world reality

Think of it as designing the shape of your life, with money as a tool that helps you build it.

WHY "BUDGETS" ARE BORING

For a lot of people, the word "budget" has the same effect as elevator music; it causes instant glaze-over, mild dread, and a sudden urge to do anything else. That's because "budgeting" often feels like punishment, restriction, rules, and no-fun money. But here's the secret: *A budget is just a plan for your money.* That's it. Nothing scary, nothing boring, nothing designed to squash your life.

So, call it something that resonates with you. Some people prefer these terms:

Adventure Plan—For the travellers saving for flights, trips, international food tours, and "I'm in a new country!" moments.

Freedom Plan—For people who crave choice, independence, and a life that isn't dictated by bills.

Know Your Numbers—Simple, clear, calm, perfect if you like tidy things.

Know Where It Goes—Soft, non-judgmental, and surprisingly motivating.

Money Map—A gentle guide that helps you get from "here" to "where you want to be."

When the name feels right, the plan feels right, so call it whatever makes you want to stick with it.

A QUICK LOOK AT THE FIRE MOVEMENT (FINANCIAL INDEPENDENCE, RETIRE EARLY)

You might have heard whispers about the FIRE movement, a lifestyle many people follow because they want one thing: Freedom.

Not the freedom to stop working at 35 (though some aim for that), but more freedom to choose:

- when to work
- how much to work
- what kind of work feels meaningful
- and how to build a life not dominated by money stress

How FIRE Works

At its heart, FIRE is built on three pillars:

1. Frugality—spending intentionally

Not deprivation. Not being cheap. Just choosing not to spend on things that don't matter to you.

2. Saving and investing aggressively

Because the more you save and invest early, the sooner your investments start paying you instead of the other way around.

3. Building passive income

Through index funds, super, long-term investing, or side hustles. Some FIRE followers want to fully retire early. Others want "work optional" living. Some just want financial breathing room and a simpler life.

FIRE isn't a rigid lifestyle—it's a spectrum. And it's absolutely optional.

What FIRE Teaches Everyone

Even if you never want extreme frugality or early retirement, the core lessons are gold:

- Spend on what matters
- Cut what doesn't
- Invest consistently
- Build long-term security
- Choose a life on purpose

FIRE reminds you that money is a tool for freedom, not something that should control you.

> **SMART TIP**
>
> *Call your money plan something that inspires you enough to stick with it.*

START WITH YOUR VALUES

Your plan begins with the things that matter most to you, not what society tells you should matter.

Ask yourself the question, *Do I value:*

- Freedom?
- Stability?
- Family?
- Travel?
- Creativity?
- Study?
- Health?
- Contribution?
- Adventure?
- Income?
- Security?
- Time?

Knowing your values helps you stay true to yourself when making decisions.

Money flows much better when it aligns with who you are.

FOUR BUILDING BLOCKS OF A SMART PLAN

Your plan has four layers that are all simple, flexible, and powerful.

1. Daily and Weekly Habits

These are your foundations. They shape your financial life gently and consistently.

Examples:

- using the bucket system
- checking your account once a week
- packing lunch instead of buying it
- reviewing subscriptions

- tracking savings for a goal
- avoiding impulse shopping
- doing a monthly "money tidy-up"

Small habits make large differences.

2. Short-Term Goals (0–12 Months)

These keep life fun and motivating.

Examples:

- a concert
- a new laptop
- a weekend trip
- building a small emergency buffer
- paying off a mini loan
- saving for something meaningful

Short-term goals keep your energy high and your momentum strong.

3. Medium-Term Goals (1–5 Years)

These shape your lifestyle and choices.

Examples:

- buying a car
- studying or retraining
- travelling overseas
- moving out
- saving for something substantial
- starting a business

Medium-term goals help you make decisions that support where you want to be next.

4. Long-Term Goals (5+ Years)

These are about building a future you're proud of.

Examples:

- home ownership
- financial independence
- major travel
- investing goals
- career milestones
- long-term savings
- building wealth for security

These goals become your North Star, guiding your big decisions without locking you in. The four building blocks give you structure. The next section helps you to personalise them.

SMART TIP

Your money plan shouldn't feel strict. It should feel supportive.

ACTIVITY: YOUR FIRST MONEY MAP

Let's put everything into a simple structure you can update anytime. Fill in these prompts:

1. **My Values:** (Write 3–5 things that matter most)

____

____

____

2. **My Top Short-Term Goal:** (What do you want in the next 12 months?)

____

3. **My Medium-Term Goal:** (What do you want in the next 1–5 years?)

4. **My Long-Term Vision:** (What life do you want 5–10+ years from now?)

5. **My Action Habits:** (List 3 habits to support your goals)

6. **My Money Safety Rules:** (Set your boundaries)

7. **My Bucket Plan:** (Spend / Save / Grow / Give)

____

____

____

8. **My Investing Plan:** (Where you're putting your long-term money)

____

____

____

9. **My Super Plan:** (Know your fund, fees, contributions and investment choice)

____

____

____

10. **My Protection Plan:** (Personal insurance, contents, travel, devices etc.)

____

____

____

This becomes your personal guide — simple, clear, powerful.

PLANNING WITHOUT PRESSURE

Someone once wrote a five-year plan that looked neat and perfect. Life, of course, moved on, and they ignored it completely. But when they looked back, they realised something interesting: They still hit many of the milestones, not because the plan forced them, but because the plan gave them clarity about what mattered.

The details changed. The direction didn't.

A good money plan gives guidance, not guilt.

> **SMART TIP**
>
> *A small check-in can keep a small slip-up from becoming a big setback.*

HOW TO KEEP YOUR PLAN ALIVE

Your plan shouldn't sit in a drawer.

Check in every few months:

- Has my situation changed?
- Have my goals changed?
- Have my values changed?
- Do I need to adjust anything?

Life happens. Plans evolve. You grow. That's the whole point.

SMART TIP

Review your plan when life changes, not on a fixed schedule.

THE POWER OF AN ACCOUNTABILITY BUDDY

Often habits are easier when you don't do them alone. You may have study buddies, or gym buddies, and you can absolutely have a money buddy too—someone who helps you stay on track, reminds you of your goals, and celebrates the wins with you.

It could be:

- a friend
- a sibling
- a cousin
- a partner
- a parent, aunt, uncle, trusted relation
- someone who wants to "get their money sorted"

It's not about judging each other's choices. They don't suddenly become the spending police. It's about supporting each other's direction.

A good accountability buddy:

- checks in with you (weekly or fortnightly)
- helps you talk through tricky decisions
- reminds you what you said you wanted
- keeps you honest about impulse spending
- shares their own goals so you're both learning
- celebrates your progress, not your perfection

The right buddy makes financial growth feel less lonely and way more fun.

BUDDY CHECKS

Chris and Jo are two friends who decided to start checking in every Sunday afternoon, for just a quick, ten minute chat: "How'd you go with your savings this week?" They didn't lecture each other, they just shared. Within a few months, they'd both built habits neither of them could stick to alone.

Sometimes, the thing you need most is simply someone else walking in the same direction.

FUTURE YOU WILL THANK YOU

Creating a money plan isn't about being perfect, it's about building a life you feel proud of, free from unnecessary stress. The habits you build now will shape your:

- confidence
- choices
- opportunities
- independence
- lifestyle
- security
- future freedom

Money is a tool. You are the architect. And you're building something truly worthwhile.

WHAT'S NEXT?

Up next, we have: **SMART Tech: Thrive With Money in a Digital World**.

Now that you have a money plan, the next challenge is protecting it in a world that never stops scrolling.

Technology shapes almost every part of how we live, learn, and manage money, sometimes in ways we don't even notice. From the apps we use to track spending, to the platforms we trust with our banking, to the way information moves online, tech can make life easier... or a lot more complicated.

SMART Tech is about understanding the digital tools around you, so you stay in control instead of feeling overwhelmed or influenced by whatever pops up on your screen. You don't need to be a coder or a "tech person" to use tech well. You just need to know how the systems work, how they make money, and how to protect yourself while you're using them.

This chapter helps you navigate the digital world with clarity: the apps worth trusting, the ones to avoid, the settings that keep you safe, and the habits that make your online life smoother and smarter.

Tech isn't the enemy. But it's not automatically your friend either. *SMART Tech* helps you use it as a tool, not a trap.

CHAPTER 17

SMART TECH

"Technology is a useful servant but a dangerous master."

—Christian Lous Lange

SMART Tech: Thrive With Money in a Digital World

> *"Smart tools are useful. Smart thinking is essential."*

Money used to live in wallets, purses, and bank branches. Now it lives in your pocket, on your phone, inside apps, and across platforms you don't even realise are tracking you. It's faster, more convenient, and it's also easier than ever to overspend, get trapped in subscriptions, or fall into digital money tricks designed by people who really understand human psychology.

This chapter shows you how to stay in control by using tech to your advantage instead of letting it quietly drain your bank account (or your sanity).

YOUR PHONE: YOUR BEST FINANCIAL TOOL... OR YOUR WORST?

You can use your phone to:

- send money instantly
- track your spending
- save automatically
- pay bills
- manage subscriptions
- remind you of due dates
- help you invest
- protect your identity

It can also:

- encourage impulse purchases
- hide subscription traps
- collect your data
- track your patterns
- target you with ads that hit your weaknesses
- make "tap and go" feel painless
- distract you from your financial goals

Your phone isn't the problem, it is simply a tool, and this chapter teaches you how to use it like a pro.

DIGITAL WALLETS, AUTO-PAY, AND TAP-AND-GO: THE INVISIBLE SPENDING TRAP

Digital payments feel frictionless, which is exactly why it's easy to overspend without noticing.

Tap. Swipe. PayID. Apple Pay. "Double click to confirm."

How to stay in control:

- Turn on bank notifications so you see every transaction instantly
- Check your transactions weekly
- Put a spending limit on your digital card
- Keep large purchases in a separate account so you don't "tap by accident"
- Use a debit card instead of credit to stay honest

Convenience is amazing but awareness is better.

SMART TIP

If you forgot you had it, you don't need it.

SUBSCRIPTIONS: MONEY-LEAKING NINJAS

Subscriptions are the new sneaky money trap. It's easy to accumulate subscriptions without realising you've accidentally built an entire monthly mini mortgage on:

- Spotify
- Netflix
- Apple Music
- cloud storage
- beauty boxes
- game passes
- photo editing apps
- language apps
- streaming
- fitness apps
- crypto or trading tools
- random "trial" apps from a late-night download

How to find your hidden charges:

Apple users: Settings → Your Name → Subscriptions

Android users: Google Play → Profile → Payments & Subscriptions

Look at everything. Cancel ruthlessly.

IDENTITY THEFT: FINANCIAL RISK NOBODY TALKS ABOUT

Young people are the perfect target for identity theft because you:

- reuse passwords
- post your life online
- connect to public Wi-Fi
- don't lock your SIM
- don't realise how valuable your identity is

If someone steals your identity, they can, without you even realising at first:

- open accounts in your name
- sign up for loans
- ruin your credit score
- access your bank accounts
- take over your social media
- impersonate you

How to protect yourself easily:

- use strong, unique passwords
- use a password manager
- turn on two-factor authentication (2FA)
- don't share code-verification screenshots
- lock your SIM with a PIN
- avoid logging into banking on public Wi-Fi
- delete old accounts you don't use

Your online safety is your financial safety.

ALGORITHMS: HOW SOCIALS HELP YOU SPEND

Social media knows:

- when you're bored
- when you're tired
- when you're emotional
- what products your friends buy
- what makes you click
- what "look" you want
- what you've been Googling at 1 am

Ads aren't random, they're personalised psychological nudges.

When you see the "perfect thing" at the "perfect time," that's not coincidence, it's by design.

How to break the spell:

- Wait 24 hours before buying anything you saw in an ad
- Ask "Would I want this if I hadn't seen the ad?"
- Don't shop when emotional
- Clear your browsing history
- Use limits or screen-time blocks

> **SMART TIP**
>
> *Impulse buys are often emotions pretending to be decisions.*

EMOTIONAL SPENDING AND DOPAMINE

Money decisions don't just happen in your wallet, they happen in your brain first. When you see something you want, your brain releases a chemical called dopamine. It's the same spark you feel when someone compliments you, you get good news, or your favourite person texts back. Dopamine feels exciting, rewarding... and it tricks your brain into thinking you have to have the thing right now.

Online stores and social media platforms know this. That's why they use:

- limited-time countdowns
- "Only 2 left!" warnings
- flash sales
- personalised ads
- recommendations based on what you've been Googling
- bright colours and fast checkout screens

These are psychological nudges designed to keep the dopamine flowing. This is why impulse buying feels amazing in the moment... and annoying later. But here's the good news: you don't need superhuman willpower, you just need a pause button.

Dopamine isn't bad, it just needs supervision. The 24-hour rule works because it lets your dopamine settle so your logical brain can catch up. If you still want it tomorrow, great. If the feeling disappears? Congratulations!! You just dodged an emotional purchase.

SMART TIP

If something feels urgent, emotional, or "too perfect," your dopamine is doing the talking. Give it a day to let your brain and your budget breathe.

ONLINE SHOPPING: BE SAFE, SMART, AND SCAM-FREE

If you shop online (and who doesn't?), follow these rules:

Before buying:

- Check the website reviews
- Look for a real return policy
- Make sure the site starts with *https://*
- Avoid deals that look unbelievable
- Prefer PayPal for buyer protection
- Don't send bank transfers to strangers

When selling:

- Never share your home address
- Meet in busy places
- Don't accept weird payment requests
- Watch out for fake courier scams

Online bargains are great as long as you're smarter than the scammer.

SIDE HUSTLES IN A DIGITAL AGE: USING TECH TO EARN

This generation is bursting with digital earning options:

- editing videos for creators
- managing social media for small businesses
- selling clothes on Depop or Vinted
- digital art commissions
- tutoring online
- making Canva templates
- reselling items

- recording voiceovers
- building websites
- flipping vintage items
- streaming or content creation
- pet-sitting apps

SMART TIP

If you have a skill, the internet has a marketplace for it.

INFLUENCERS, LIFESTYLE PRESSURE, AND MONEY FOMO

Social media is a highlight reel, it is not reality.

Influencers:

- are paid to promote
- receive freebies
- borrow luxury items
- stage photos
- use filters
- curate a lifestyle for "the aesthetic"

Comparing your real life to someone's digital fiction is unfair, and expensive.

How to stay grounded:

- Ask "Is this real or curated?"
- Remember that influencers are paid to persuade you
- Follow creators who inspire healthy habits, not "spend for the vibe" lifestyles

You don't need a perfect feed. You need a stable bank account. Influencers sell aspiration. You're building a real life.

AI CAN GIVE YOU ANSWERS. IT CAN'T GIVE YOU JUDGMENT.

Tools like ChatGPT can be incredibly useful for learning about investing, comparing options, or understanding new concepts. But they don't know your goals, your risk tolerance, or your personal situation.

Use AI to ask better questions, not to blindly follow answers. Try prompts like:

- "Explain this investment in simple terms"
- "What are the risks I should understand?"
- "What would make this a bad investment?"
- "Who benefits most from this product?"

Smart investors don't outsource thinking. They use tools to build understanding, then make decisions with clarity and confidence.

> **SMART TIP**
>
> *If an AI answer makes something sound "too easy" or "guaranteed," that's your cue to slow down, not speed up.*

CYBER SAFETY MEETS MONEY SAFETY

Here's what every financially confident young adult needs:

- Two-factor authentication

- Secure passwords
- Fraud alerts enabled
- Bank notifications
- Awareness of phishing
- Safe online marketplace habits
- Subscription checks
- Scam awareness
- Clear boundaries in DMs
- Confidence to say "no"

This isn't paranoia. This is modern life.

LET'S REVISIT THE FIRE MOVEMENT

We touched on FIRE earlier, but here's how tech fits. Tech makes FIRE easier because:

- budgeting apps track spending
- investment apps automate investing
- comparison sites help you choose better deals
- income tools help you freelance
- online communities share advice
- automation removes emotional decision-making

FIRE isn't about being cheap, t's about being intentional. You don't have to live like a monk, you just need to understand your money flow—and tech helps you do that effortlessly.

SMART TIP

If your phone is always with you, let it work for you, not against you.

THE PHONE THAT SAVED, NOT SPENT

Jenna once used her phone mostly for shopping, games and streaming. She constantly wondered why her money disappeared. Then, she:

- turned on spending alerts
- set up two savings buckets
- added bill reminders
- canceled four subscriptions
- put big purchases on a 48-hour waitlist
- changed three passwords.

And suddenly? Money stopped leaking. Not because she earned more, but because her phone stopped quietly sabotaging her goals.

Your phone can be a financial sinkhole or it can be your strongest money system. You choose how it behaves.

WHAT'S NEXT?

Money doesn't exist in a vacuum. It's connected to your friendships, habits, choices, well-being, and the way you show up in the world.

SMART Life is all about stepping back and understanding that the life you build, the everyday decisions, the people you surround yourself with, and the boundaries you set, have as much impact on your future as any pay or investment. This chapter helps you get clear on what matters to you, and how to shape a lifestyle that supports your goals instead of working against them. It's not about perfection or rigid routines. It's about creating a life that feels good now *and* builds the future you imagine for yourself.

Up Next: **SMART Life: Design The Life You Want.**

CHAPTER 18

SMART LIFE

"Decide the kind of life you want, then say no to everything that isn't it."

—Unknown

SMART Life: Design The Life You Want

> *"Money is simply a tool. Use it to build a life you are proud to live."*

You've done something remarkable. You've read, learned, reflected, questioned, laughed, nodded, and probably had a few "Why did nobody tell me this earlier?" moments along the way. That's the heart of this whole book—sharing the tools, ideas and habits that make life clearer, calmer and more in your control. Not perfect. Not rigid. Just yours.

You now understand things most adults wish they'd been taught sooner: How money works, how to earn it, grow it, protect it, plan with it, and use it with intention instead of confusion. And that puts you miles ahead.

YOU DON'T NEED TO GET EVERYTHING RIGHT

Let's say this clearly: You're not meant to be perfect at money. Nobody is.

You don't need to track every dollar, invest like a professional, or have a flawless plan. You just need awareness, a few good habits, a sense of direction and the confidence to ask questions.

Every chapter in this book gives you one more tool, but the real power comes from using even one of them consistently.

Small choices → big results.

YOUR NEXT STEPS (THE GENTLE VERSION)

There's no "one right order," but here's a simple guideline for what to do next:

1. Choose one habit to start this week

Maybe it's checking your bank account weekly, or setting up a bucket system, or reviewing your superannuation.

Just one.

2. Choose one short-term goal to work toward

A few hundred dollars saved for something that matters is a great start.

3. Create your Money Map

Use the template from the SMART Money chapter. Make it messy. Make it honest. Make it yours.

4. Talk to someone you trust

Money conversations feel better when they're shared with someone you trust, like a friend, parent, mentor, or "money buddy."

5. Review your plan whenever life changes

New job? Moving out? Relationship shift? New goal? Your plan grows with you.

A FEW TRUTHS

Money doesn't buy happiness, but it does buy options: Security feels better than stress. Prepared feels better than panicked. (And preparation doesn't have to be complicated.) Steady feels better than scattered.

You are capable of being good with money, not because you know everything yet, but because you're willing to learn. That willingness is rare, and unbelievably powerful.

MINDSET MATTERS

Tom looked at his bank balance, laughed bitterly, and said, "Money and I just don't get along."

Years later, after learning, practising small habits, and getting clear on what mattered to him, his entire life changed: more confidence, better decisions, fewer surprises, more opportunities, more control.

When asked what made the difference, he said: "I stopped assuming I was bad with money and decided to get curious instead."

Curiosity is your superpower. Use it freely.

YOUR SMART LIFE IS WAITING

You don't have to build it all today.
You don't have to rush.
You don't have to follow anyone else's path.

Just start where you are.
Use what you have.
Take one step.
Then another.

You've already done the hardest part—you paid attention. The rest gets easier from here. Future You is already smiling and so proud of you right now.

> **SMART TIP**
> *Money skills grow the same way muscles do—one small, consistent action at a time.*

WHAT'S NEXT?

This book isn't something you "finish" and move on from. It's something you come back to. When life changes, when money feels confusing again, or when you're ready for the next step.

The **SMART** series of books is underway, and while future titles are being developed, the most important work starts now: Use what you've learned in your own life, in your own way.

Money is a lifelong relationship. It evolves as you grow, earn, study, travel, work, love, and change direction. You don't need more information right now. You need practice, curiosity, and confidence. And you already have all three.

You're not behind.
You're not late.
You're right on time.

Money is a lifelong relationship.
You've just learned how to have a healthy one.

You might have read this book from cover to cover and not done a single exercise. That's okay. Why not pick just one now and get started?

30-DAY SMART CHALLENGE

Build Your Confidence. Build Your Money Muscles.

Think of this challenge as a month-long "money fitness circuit"—small actions that make a big difference over time.

Nothing intense. Nothing judgemental. Just simple steps that help you build awareness, control and confidence.

You can start on any day.
You can go in order or skip around.
You can do it with a friend (accountability buddies make this way more fun).

Let's get started.

DAY 1 — KNOW YOUR NUMBERS
Check your bank balance and write down:

- what came in
- what went out
- what surprised you

Awareness is power.

DAY 2 — SET ONE TINY MONEY GOAL
Something you can achieve in 30 days — like saving $50 or cancelling a subscription.

DAY 3 — CREATE YOUR BUCKETS
Spend, Save, Grow, Give. Name them in your banking app.

DAY 4 — REVIEW SUBSCRIPTIONS
Cancel one thing you don't use or don't need.

DAY 5 — TURN ON PHONE ALERTS
Activate bank notifications so every tap shows instantly.

DAY 6 — CHANGE ONE PASSWORD
Especially for banking or email. Make it strong.

DAY 7 — DO A MINI AUDIT
Check for:

- unused apps
- auto-renew trials
- sneaky in-app purchases

Clear out the clutter.

DAY 8 — SAVE $10 AUTOMATICALLY
Set up a recurring transfer to your Save or Grow bucket. Small habits build big results.

DAY 9 — LEARN YOUR SUPER FUND'S NAME
Yes, really. Look it up in MyGov. Knowing is step one.

DAY 10 — CHECK YOUR EMPLOYER IS PAYING SUPER
It takes one minute on MyGov. Tick that box for future-you.

DAY 11 — CHOOSE YOUR "MONEY PLAN" NAME
Adventure Plan, Freedom Plan, Money Map, whatever resonates.

DAY 12 — DECLUTTER YOUR FEED
Unfollow 3 accounts that make you want to impulse-buy or feel "less." Keep the inspiration, ditch the pressure.

DAY 13 — LEARN ONE INVESTING TERM
ETF, index fund, diversification—pick one. Write a short definition.

DAY 14 — PRACTICE A 24-HOUR WAIT
See something you want? Pause. Give it a day. See how you feel tomorrow.

DAY 15 — TALK ABOUT MONEY WITH SOMEONE YOU TRUST
A friend, parent, partner—just a simple chat.

DAY 16 — CHECK YOUR PHONE'S SECURITY
Enable:

- 2FA
- SIM PIN
- biometric login
- screen lock

Goodbye, identity theft.

DAY 17 — PLAN ONE LOW-COST FUN ACTIVITY
A picnic, a movie night at home, a hike. Fun doesn't require spending.

DAY 18 — LIST YOUR MONTHLY "NON-NEGOTIABLES"
Phone bill, transport, lunches, hobbies. Know your baseline cost of living.

DAY 19 — REVIEW YOUR PAY SLIP
Check that tax and super look right. You'd be amazed how many people never do this.

DAY 20 — CLEAN OUT YOUR WALLET / BAG / BACKPACK
Old receipts, random coins, loyalty cards. A tidy space creates a tidy mind.

DAY 21 — LEARN ONE SCAM TO WATCH FOR
Grandparent scam, phishing, marketplace scams—knowledge is protection.

DAY 22 — ADD A MONEY QUOTE TO YOUR LOCK SCREEN
Something positive, not pressure-filled. Keep inspiration front and centre.

DAY 23 — CHECK YOUR BANK FEES
See what you're paying—and whether switching accounts could save money.

DAY 24 — MAKE A SMART GOAL
Specific, Measurable, Achievable, Relevant, Time-bound. Choose something meaningful.

DAY 25 — CREATE YOUR FIRST "MONEY MAP" PAGE
Use the template from Chapter 14. Make it messy. Make it real.

DAY 26 — DO ONE THING FOR "FUTURE YOU"
Add $5 to super, update a password, tidy your desk, create a savings pocket. Small but powerful.

DAY 27 — PRACTICE A NO-SPEND DAY
One day. Zero unnecessary purchases. A reset for your brain (and your bank).

DAY 28 — DO A TECH SAFETY SWEEP

- Update apps.
- Review permissions.
- Remove apps that track your location unnecessarily.

DAY 29 — CELEBRATE ONE WIN
Something you did this month—big or tiny—that moved you forward.

DAY 30 — REFLECT

- What did you learn?
- What felt easy?
- What surprised you?
- What do you want to keep doing?

Confidence grows by doing—and you've just done a whole month.

Resources

HELPFUL TOOLS, LINKS, AND PLACES TO LEARN MORE

These are trustworthy, practical sources your readers can return to anytime they want to build confidence with money, life admin, investing, and staying safe online. (Where relevant, these are Australian-specific.)

Money, Banking, and Financial Literacy

MoneySmart (ASIC)

Simple, reliable information on budgeting, saving, investing, super, loans, and avoiding scams. Great calculators and "real-people" examples.
www.moneysmart.gov.au

CHOICE

Independent product reviews. Helps you compare things like appliances, health insurance, and even shopping platforms.
www.choice.com.au

Finder / Canstar / RateCity

Comparison websites for:

- savings accounts
- home loans
- Insurance
- investment platforms
- credit cards

Use them for research, not gospel. Compare carefully.

Superannuation and Work

ATO — Superannuation and Tax

How to apply for a TFN, understand tax, check if your boss is paying super, track lost super and learn about contributions.
www.ato.gov.au

MyGov

Connects to your ATO and super accounts. Essential for keeping track of your money and work records.
www.mygov.au

Investing and Markets

ASX (Australian Securities Exchange)

Company info, investor education, and explanations of shares, ETFs and how markets work.
www.asx.com.au

Morningstar (Free Articles)

Independent investment research, including basic fund info.
www.morningstar.com.au

Vanguard / Betashares / iShares (ETF Providers)

Great beginner learning resources about index investing, diversification and fees.

Budgeting and Money Management Apps

(Australian-friendly ones)

- **PocketSmith** – calendar-style budgeting
- **Up Bank** – built-in tools for spending insights
- **WeMoney** – financial wellness + savings goals
- **Frollo** – track spending across accounts
- **Raiz** – round-up investing for beginners
- **Spaceship** – simple app-based investing

Your phone can be a personal CFO if you let it.

Cyber Safety and Scam Prevention

Scamwatch

Up-to-date scam alerts, reporting, and safety guides.
www.scamwatch.gov.au

ReportCyber

Report hacks, identity theft, phishing and online fraud.
www.cyber.gov.au/report

eSafety Commissioner

Essential for online safety, bullying, digital identity protection and handling online conflict.
www.esafety.gov.au

Work, Study, and Earning

Fair Work Ombudsman

Check pay rates, work rights, penalty rates and workplace rules.
www.fairwork.gov.au

Seek / Indeed / Jora

Job-search and resume tools.

TAFE and University Course Finders

For exploring future study paths and HECS-HELP info.

Mental Health Support

Money stress is real. If you ever feel overwhelmed, these are safe places to talk:

- **Headspace** – headspace.org.au
- **Lifeline** – 13 11 14
- **Kids Helpline** – kidshelpline.com.au / 1800 55 1800
- **Beyond Blue** – beyondblue.org.au

Financial wellbeing includes emotional wellbeing.

SMART TIP

Use resources that make you feel informed, not overwhelmed.

Glossary

MONEY TERMS IN PLAIN ENGLISH

Account Balance: How much money is currently in your bank account.

Afterpay / Buy Now Pay Later (BNPL): A way to buy something now and pay it off over weeks. Convenient but risky—late fees add up fast and it affects borrowing ability.

Algorithm: The "brain" behind apps that decides what content you see and what ads appear, based on your behaviour.

Asset: Something you own that has value, like money, shares, property, or a business.

ATM (Automatic Teller Machine): A machine where you can take out cash or check your balance.

Budget: A plan for where your money goes. You can call it your Adventure Plan, Freedom Plan, Money Map—whatever makes sense to you.

Buyers Protection: A service (like PayPal) that helps refund you when sellers fail to deliver goods.

Compound Interest: Interest earning interest. One of the most powerful forces in building wealth.

Credit Score: A number that shows how trustworthy you are with money. Helps banks decide if they'll lend to you.

Debit Card: Linked to your own money. When you spend, it comes directly from your account.

Diversification: Not putting all your eggs in one basket. Spreading investments across different areas.

Emergency Fund: Money saved for unexpected events, like repairs, bills or lost income.

ETF (Exchange-Traded Fund): A simple bundle of investments, often tracking an index. Great for beginners.

Frugal/Frugality: Choosing to spend intentionally on what matters and cut back on what doesn't.

HECS-HELP: Australia's student loan system—you borrow for study and repay through tax once you earn enough.

Identity Theft: When someone steals your personal info and pretends to be you to access money or credit.

Index Fund: A low-cost investment that simply follows the market instead of trying to beat it.

Interest Rate: The cost of borrowing money, or the reward for saving money.

Investment: Money you put somewhere expecting it to grow over time.

Liability: Money you owe—debts, loans, credit cards.

PayID: Instant transfer payment system using your phone number or email.

Phishing: Fake emails, messages, or websites trying to trick you into giving personal details.

Portfolio: Your collection of investments.

Return: How much you make (or lose) on an investment.

Risk: The possibility your money might go down, not just up.

Salary Sacrifice: An arrangement where your employer puts some of your pay into super before tax.

Scam: A trick to steal your money or identity. Often looks convincing.

Shares / Stocks: Small pieces of a company that you can buy.

Side Hustle: Any small way of earning extra money, usually outside your main job.

SIM Swap Scam: A scam where someone takes over your phone number, giving them access to your accounts—fixable by locking your SIM with a PIN.

Superannuation (Super): Your long-term retirement savings account. Employers must pay into it.

Tax File Number (TFN): Your personal number for the ATO—needed for jobs, banking and study.

Two-Factor Authentication (2FA): A second layer of security (like a code sent to your phone).

Withdrawal: Money moved out of your account.

Quotes and Sources

Some of the quotations included throughout this book come from well-known authors and thinkers whose ideas about habits, learning, and decision-making continue to influence how we approach money and life. The following works are referenced in connection with those quotations.

Buffett, Warren E. *The Essays of Warren Buffett: Lessons for Corporate America*. 4th ed. Omaha, NE: Carolina Academic Press, 2013.

Huffington, Arianna. "Burnout: Time to Abandon a Very Costly Collective Delusion." *The Huffington Post*, March 19, 2014. https://www.huffpost.com/entry/burnout_b_5102468.

Aristotle. *Nicomachean Ethics*. Translated by W. D. Ross. Oxford: Oxford University Press, 1925.

Durant, Will. *The Story of Philosophy: The Lives and Opinions of the World's Greatest Philosophers*. New York: Simon & Schuster, 1926.

Franklin, Benjamin. *The Way to Wealth*. 1758.

Franklin, Benjamin. *Poor Richard's Almanack*. Philadelphia: Benjamin Franklin, 1732–1758.

Kennedy, John F. "Special Message to the Congress on the State of the Union." January 14, 1963.

Lamott, Anne. *Bird by Bird: Some Instructions on Writing and Life*. New York: Anchor Books, 1994.

Lee, Stan, and Steve Ditko. *Amazing Fantasy*, no. 15. New York: Marvel Comics, 1962.

Mecham, Jesse. *You Need a Budget: The Proven System for Breaking the Paycheck-to-Paycheck Cycle, Getting Out of Debt, and Living the Life You Want*. New York: Harper Business, 2017.

Milliman, Ronald E. "Using Background Music to Affect the Behavior of Supermarket Shoppers." *Journal of Marketing* 46, no. 3 (Summer 1982): 86–91. https://doi.org/10.1177/002224298204600313.

Parliament of Australia. *House of Representatives Hansard*. February 13, 2023. Canberra: Parliament of Australia. Hansard transcript.

Sharma, Robin. *The 5 AM Club: Own Your Morning. Elevate Your Life*. Toronto: HarperCollins Canada, 2018.

Twain, Mark. *Pudd'nhead Wilson's New Calendar*. Hartford, CT: American Publishing Company, 1897.

Some quotations in the book are widely shared sayings or proverbs whose original sources cannot be reliably identified. These are attributed as "Unknown."

Acknowledgements

A project like this doesn't happen alone.

Thank you to my family, Matt, Mitch, and Maddy, for your patience (most of the time), humour (sometimes), and unwavering support (all the time) even if you'll never read this.

Thanks also to my clients and community, who inspire me every day with their questions, curiosity, and courage.

And to the brilliant minds who shaped the conversations, insights, and stories throughout this book.

Finally, heartfelt appreciation to everyone working to build financial literacy in young people.

May your impact ripples for generations.

About the Author

Amanda Cassar, MFP, C.Dec, SSA™ SAPEPAA™ is an Australian financial adviser, author and educator who has spent decades helping people make smarter decisions about money. She is the founder of Wealth Planning Partners and Trusted Aged Care Services and is widely recognised for her work in financial literacy, consumer protection, and advocacy for vulnerable clients.

Amanda is the author of *Financial Secrets Revealed* and the creator of the *SMART Money* series, which is designed to help young people build practical money skills for real life. She also hosts the *Financial Secrets Revealed* podcast, where she shares conversations and insights about money, life, and the choices that shape our financial futures.

Through her writing, speaking, and advisory work, Amanda's goal is simple: to make complex financial topics clearer, more practical, and easier for people to navigate with confidence.

www.ingramcontent.com/pod-product-compliance
Lightning Source LLC
La Vergne TN
LVHW022202200926
848481LV00006B/1819